ESTRENO Collection of Contemporary Spanish Plays

General Editor: Martha T. Halsey

A LOVE TOO BEAUTIFUL

MANUEL MARTÍNEZ MEDIERO

A LOVE TOO BEAUTIFUL
The Story of Joanna of Castile

(Juana del amor hermoso)

Translated by Hazel Cazorla

ESTRENO
University Park, Pennsylvania
1995

ESTRENO Contemporary Spanish Plays 8
General Editor: Martha T. Halsey
Department of Spanish, Italian and Portuguese
College of the Liberal Arts
The Pennsylvania State University
University Park PA 16802 USA

Cataloging Data
Martínez Mediero, Manuel, 1939-
A Love Too Beautiful
Translation of: Juana del amor hermoso
Contents: A Love Too Beautiful
I. Cazorla, Hazel. II. Title
Library of Congress Catalog Card No.: 94-61737
ISBN: 0-9631212-7-8

This edition has been translated
with the financial assistance of the
Spanish Dirección General del Libro y Bibliotecas
of the Ministerio de Cultura

Cover: Jeffrey Eads

A NOTE ON THE PLAY

A Love Too Beautiful, a fantastical drama set in the dark heart of the Spanish court of Isabella and Ferdinand, plays like a surrealistic thriller—filled with mystery and romance, political intrigue, ghosts, torture, buffonery, and betrayal. Yet, at the center of the action, is a very real—and strikingly modern—woman, Joanna of Castile.

Here emerges so powerful a portrait of "Joanna the Mad" that it gives psychological form to what would otherwise be a puzzling cavalcade of historical moments. In fact, the play by Manuel Martínez Mediero sets forth so persuasive a sequence of events that history comes alive. And the elegant and restrained style of the translation by Hazel Cazorla gives the characters archetypal importance.

A Love Too Beautiful is a director's dream—it demands bravura performances and dazzling staging. And the audience will be stunned by the paradoxical strangeness of historic truth, as it is set against the power of poetic action in *A Love Too Beautiful*.

> Judy Kelly
> Professor Drama, University of Dallas
> Producer/Director of Theater, Opera and Television
> University of Dallas and PBS

MANUEL MARTÍNEZ MEDIERO

ABOUT THE PLAYWRIGHT

Born in 1939 in Badajoz, a provincial city in the region of Extremadura, Spain, Manuel Martínez Mediero went off to the nation's capital in 1960 to study for a degree in economics at the University of Madrid, where he also became interested in writing for the stage. During the sixties he spent some time in Barcelona and Bilbao, becoming associated with the semi-clandestine world of protest theater at that time. At the famous Festival of Sitges in 1969 he won the first of his many theater awards, going on to acquire critical prestige, among an élite, as an avant-garde writer with a highly critical social and political message for his times. Since 1970 he has resided mainly in Badajoz, earning his living as an economist but continuing to write continuously for the stage.

Fame, one might even call it notoriety, burst upon him in 1975 with the staging of *Las hermanas de Búfalo Bill* ("Buffalo Bill's Sisters"), an event which coincided with the death of the aged Spanish dictator, Franco, who had ruled for almost forty years. The public and critics thronged to see the play since word quickly spread that it was a hilarious lampooning of the late Generalísimo. Reaction from the political right wing was immediate and extreme. One newspaper called it an "affront to national honor;" while reactionary groups made threats against the author and the company. During one performance someone even threw a smoke bomb into the theater. All this publicity assured the play a resounding *succès de scandale*: it ran for over five hundred performances.

Among the best known of Martínez Mediero's works are: *El convidado* (*The Guest, 1968*), an intense one-act piece of 'theater of cruelty,' *El último gallinero* ("The Last Chicken Roost," 1969), an animal allegory, and *El bebé furioso* ("The Furious Baby," 1974), the first commercially successful absurdist play by this author. *Las planchadoras* ("The Laundresses," 1971, staged 1978) examines the sexual opression of women in a paternalistic society, a theme which recurs in *Lisístrata* ("Lysistrata," 1980), a reworking of the classical comedy by Aristophanes, in *Fedra* (1981), Mediero's version of the Senecan tragedy, and in the tragi-comic *Juana del amor hermoso* (1982), the play now translated here as *A Love Too Beautiful*, in which the author recreates the historical figure of Joanna of Castile, known as Joanna the Mad, and re-examines the mystery and intrigue hidden by the veil of her so-called madness.

ix

At the same time he gives expression to the ageless struggle of victim against persecutor, viewed from a highly contemporary feminist standpoint.

Juana del amor hermoso was first staged at the Teatro Príncipe in Madrid on February 14, 1983. Under the direction of Angel Ruggiero, it ran for over two hundred performances, starring Lola Herrera as Joanna and Emma Penella as Queen Isabella.

Juan José Otegui as Philip and Lola Herrera as Joanna, in the original 1983 production of *Juana del amor hermoso*, at the Príncipe Theater, Madrid, directed by Angel Ruggiero.

Arturo López as King Ferdinand, Vicente Parra as Archbishop Cisneros and Emma Penella as Queen Isabella, greeting the young couple, Joanna and Philip, played by Lola Herrera and Juan José Otegui in the original 1983 production in Madrid.

CHARACTERS

Joanna, heir to the throne of Castile
Isabella, Queen of Castile, Joanna's mother
Ferdinand, King of Aragon, Joanna's father
Philip the Fair, Archduke of Burgundy
Cardinal Cisneros
Friar Martin, Luis Ferrer and Marquis of Denia (All three to be played by the
    same actor)
Juan de Padilla

PERIOD

That of the characters, late fifteenth, early sixteenth century.

PART 1

The stage is bare except for an immense six-sided panel of narrow, elongated mirrors, which form the backdrop and reach up out of sight. The action begins on a darkened stage as we hear the voice of Isabella, the Catholic Queen of Castile. Myriads of tiny lights begin to twinkle from the back of the stage. The mirrors are hinged like doors to provide access for props from backstage.

ISABELLA'S VOICE: Joanna! Joanna! Where are you, Joanna? We need to have a very serious talk, my child.

JOANNA'S VOICE: Coming, Mother, coming!

(A beautiful sixteen-year old girl rushes in, very excited, holding up her skirts so as not to trip over them. In her haste she drops the letters she is carrying; so she runs back, even more excitedly if possible, to pick them up.)

JOANNA: Wait a second, Mother! I've dropped Philip's letters.

(ISABELLA does not move but waits impatiently for her daughter to come to her.)

ISABELLA: Anyone would think you had a hobgoblin behind you, Joanna! Why all this rush? Where have you been?

JOANNA: In the kitchen, Mother, reading Philip's letters out loud to Friar Martin.

ISABELLA: Heavens above! No wonder he makes so many mistakes in the kitchen accounts!

JOANNA: All the servants were there too, absolutely spellbound, as if they were in church listening to something in Latin from Cardinal Cisneros himself!

ISABELLA: Joanna, I'm not amused.

JOANNA: All the ladies' maids were going crazy over Philip's portraits.

ISABELLA: Those 'maids' are no better than a bunch of little whores.

JOANNA: We've been playing blind-man's buff all afternoon, mother!

ISABELLA: Instead of studying your Latin, which is what you should be doing, so you can impress the folks in Flanders who seem to have only two topics of conversation: cheese and tulips!

JOANNA: Mother, you mustn't forget that Flanders is where Humanism had its beginnings, right there in Rotterdam.

ISABELLA: How can you possibly compare a loud-mouth like Erasmus with our own dear Cardinal Cisneros?

JOANNA: The Cardinal's forever saying that we shall all be damned in Hell...

ISABELLA: Precisely because the people here in this Court of Castile have lost their holy fear of God.

JOANNA: Mother, I've heard ten masses this morning, one after another, just because I thought it would make you happy.

ISABELLA: Oh, I'm so glad to hear you say that! Come here, Joanna! *(She hugs her and gives her a kiss.)* How lovely you look, Joanna! I'm so afraid of losing you, my darling child.

JOANNA: Oh mother, are you crying?

ISABELLA: Even the Queen of Castile may weep sometimes, Joanna. *(Pause.)* Joanna, you do realize, don't you, that your coming marriage to the Archduke of Burgundy is a very important step for Spain?

JOANNA: And for me too, isn't it?

ISABELLA *(Speaking as both mother and politician)*: Yes, for you too, Joanna, but all of us, from the Queen to our humblest subject, must be ready to do whatever is required of us for the sake of Spain.

JOANNA: I'll do everything for love of Philip, mother. If he loves me, if I can win him, then he too will want what is best for Spain.

ISABELLA *(Not very happy with Joanna's answer)*: I'm not so sure about that, but I'm relying on you.

JOANNA: I'll carry the flag for Spain in the Netherlands, mother!

ISABELLA: But you have only two days left before you sail and you still haven't given a thought to what you're taking with you, not to mention the political instructions the King wants me to pass on to you.

JOANNA: Oh, I'm starting to feel queasy already, just thinking of having to set foot on one of those ships.

ISABELLA: Joanna, please don't make me angry. You'll be traveling to Flanders on a ship of the Spanish Fleet, with a hundred and twenty galleons to put the French in their place, if necessary.

JOANNA: You mean a hundred and twenty leaky barrels!

ISABELLA: I ought to have you whipped for saying such a thing! Where's your respect? If your father could hear you he would shed tears to think you care so little for our heritage, something so dear to our heart, and which, I might add, costs a pretty penny to maintain. Joanna, please try not to say anything offensive to the Admiral of our Invincible Armada!

JOANNA: Why can't we simply go overland through France?

ISABELLA: Through France! Never! I wouldn't dream of setting foot in France! Not even to hear Mass! Your arrival in the Netherlands must be marked properly by all the pomp and circumstance which is customary in

Spain, so that the Emperor's son will know the kind of family he is marrying into.

JOANNA: He'll probably couldn't care less about that, so long as he can see that at least I don't come with a glass eye!

ISABELLA: That is not the kind of answer I expect to hear from you. They say still waters run deep, but in your case the waters are anything but still.

JOANNA: Mother, I just know that Philip will be as handsome as he appears in his portrait.

ISABELLA: Show me. *(Pause.)* Well, your father also sent me a portrait before we were married and he certainly turned out to be less attractive in the flesh.

JOANNA: But you can't mean to compare...

ISABELLA: Oh, do be serious for a moment, Joanna! Your father and I are trying to build an Empire in the name of God and here you are, worrying over whether the Archduke has weak ankles or a squint in his left eye. Your future husband is a Catholic—I've made very sure of that—and *that* is the only kind of beauty that matters. Whatever do you think made us drive the Moslems out of Spain? There are men who are attractive because of their looks, or the perfume on their bodies, or because they know the power of the senses, and they are constantly in pursuit of pleasure and fantasies of the flesh. Trust them no further than you would a pistol-packing saint!

JOANNA: The Romans went in for their share of perfume and fantasy, but, even so, they were the ones who invented Roman Law.

ISABELLA: And what good did *that* do them?

JOANNA: Well, at least they made it possible for you politicians to do such things as put an Empire together or simply regulate the sheep industry. It was they who laid the foundations of our civilization, based on the principle of private property.

ISABELLA *(Annoyed, but determined to get the last word)*: But the Romans were the ones who assassinated Jesus Christ! And, as Cardinal Cisneros has said, God has never forgiven them for it and will condemn them to eternal punishment.

JOANNA: But Christ forgave everyone, even Judas Iscariot, and *he* was the one who really started all the trouble.

ISABELLA: Listen, my child! You may think you have the answer to everything, but I'm certainly not sending you off to the Flemish court to make a bad situation even worse; they are perverted enough already! Good heavens! Such words from this little pussy cat! Now, the Archduke

Philip *is* good-looking and he does use perfume, but he is also a Catholic, as I know from very good sources. And he likes royal ladies to be chaste, hard-working on behalf of their subjects, obedient wives, and loving mothers. Now, do you intend to ruin the whole game for your father and me?

JOANNA: All I want to do is to put a little spark into the game.

ISABELLA: Well, the day I listen to youngsters like you will be the day I see chickens pee! I can't think what we are coming to these days. *(Pause.)* In my time, marriageable young women thought only about their trousseau. But, naturally, with so much studying, so many Latin lessons, you don't have time for cooking and home-making! Although I know, of course, that Latin is the language of the future as the dear Bishop of Cordoba assures us, with his God-given foresight.

JOANNA: I'd like to send Virgil on his way with a kick in the butt!

ISABELLA *(Shocked)*: In the what?

JOANNA: In the... ankle.

ISABELLA: Ah! well, that's another matter.

JOANNA: And I've already told Don Juan de Fonseca that Mass will always be a bore until it's said in French.

ISABELLA: I can't believe what I'm hearing, Joanna! In French? You want the Holy Mass to be in French? Where did I go wrong with your education, Joanna?

JOANNA: Of course I've managed to learn a bit of French on my own, so that when I'm alone with Philip...

ISABELLA: Well, what *are* you going to say to him when you two are alone?

JOANNA *(Pause.)*: Je t'aime, je t'aime, Philipe.

(The third ("Ruhevoll") movement of Mahler's Fourth Symphony, used as the theme music for this first act, can be heard in the background. Joanna is obviously moved.)

ISABELLA: What kind of wicked words are those?

JOANNA: The ones I'm going to say to my love, the moment I set eyes on him: I love you, Philip, I love you.

ISABELLA: This can't be any child of mine! The devil himself has been at work here! *(As she says this, she raises her crucifix.)* You are no true-blooded daughter of Spain! There must be Jewish blood in your veins! Whatever will become of Spain with a future queen who speaks French like any common street-walker! Bring me some smelling salts! And a confessor! If the king ever finds out we'll never hear the last of it, and the first person to be fired will be Friar Martin. He's the one responsible for teaching you all this trash.

JOANNA: Mother, you're turning red in the face.

ISABELLA: Like the flag of Castile, you shameless girl!

JOANNA: The only reason I told you all this was to show you how happy I'm going to be.

ISABELLA: We are happy only if Spain is happy, not otherwise.

JOANNA: What am I supposed to do then?

ISABELLA: Be less happy and keep your feet on the ground. Spain has a noble task to accomplish through you. Converting Europe is our sacred destiny. The Empire cannot be achieved until all Europe prays as one beneath the joint flags of Castile and Aragon. Once *that* is a reality, then we can look forward to a new dawn of happiness, and even the Day of Judgment (which they say is about to happen anyway). We can't be truly happy until we enjoy the presence of God the Father, in Heaven.

JOANNA: But in the meantime, we can go on enjoying the small things that life offers us, can't we? Especially now that I'm going to be married and I'll be able to feel pleasure without committing mortal sin.

ISABELLA: This world is nothing but a passage to another life, Joanna.

JOANNA: But surely we can walk the passage together and love one another, beautifully, as we go. Love between a man and a woman, as equals, is the highest end to which any people can aspire. Without love, without a beautiful kind of love, there can be no children, no renovation of the human race, nothing.

ISABELLA: I seem to have stepped in just in time, thank goodness! I can't imagine what trouble you might have caused all by yourself, without any kind of direction or guidance. No, Joanna, no. You are going to marry the Archduke Philip, but not because he is good-looking or wears cologne, but because it is in the interests of Spain and most of all because Spain will not be happy until we have eliminated France. France delights in doing everything possible to give us a bad image. The French are jealous because we invented the fashion of wearing black, and above all, because we have St. James the Apostle to protect us. They envy us our other-worldliness, our martyrs and our saints, while they indulge in earthly pleasures in a society based on a market economy. And their conscience troubles them. Spain is called to high endeavors, Joanna, and you, my child, are to be our spiritual flag-bearer in the forefront of Europe.

JOANNA: Is that how you see me, Mother? As a chaste, long-suffering heroine, forever dressed in black, putting up with the indiscretions of the Archduke, whatever they may leave behind? Isn't it more honorable, and glorious even, to keep a man in his own bed by the power of love than to have him sleeping around in loveless beds of vice? What does it mean to be royal? Having to accept everything just as you do in a storm or living in exile? Why is it that politics can treat a woman's vagina like a general assembly of Parliament without any of its precious attachment to the people? Shouldn't we begin by putting our own house in order rather than dismantling so many others and leaving them all in disarray? What kind of an empire is this which refuses to look first within itself? Mother, don't you realize that nations whose ambitions outrun their limitations are destined to perish and finish up begging for what they so foolishly squandered? And yet, if you ask me to, I'll put my country before my royal rank, my duty as a daughter before my loyalty as a wife, my allegiance as a spy for Spain before my feelings as a mother. But I want you to know that I love the pleasures of this earthly life and I'm not ashamed to say so. *(Pause.)* I'll do whatever you command, and I'll do it all in the name of Castile and Aragon, in the name of Spain.

ISABELLA: I expected no less of you. You'll take sixty sets of towels with you, two hundred fine sheets, sixty blankets. In the Netherlands it gets very cold, so I've given you fifty flannel undershirts. You'll be carrying an inventory of your own jewels as well as those you'll be giving as a gift to your sister-in-law, the Archduchess Margaret, who is engaged to be married to our own dear son John. But there is something which worries me more than anything else, my dearest. You'll be entering into the state of holy matrimony, and you may be surprised, on the night of your wedding, that your husband may wish to penetrate your body with his. Accept it for the greater glory of God, who ordained that we should thus be brought into this valley of tears. And above all, don't take a bath! Bathing is a nasty French custom. Finally, though it pains me to have to tell you, there is something else that you must learn, now that you are no longer a child: Joanna, there is no Santa Claus: Santa Claus has never been anyone but the King of Aragon and I.

(Music.)

(And the music merges with the sound of waves breaking over the sides of a ship. It's very foggy. JOANNA stands in the prow of the ship, her

hair blown by the wind. At her side stands the slight figure of a young friar, carrying a huge book under his arm.)

SAILOR'S VOICE: Land ho! Land ho-o-o !

FRIAR MARTIN: We are close to land, my lady. That faint flicker of light comes from the lighthouse of Flanders.

JOANNA: Friar Martin, I don't know if all this is real, or if I'm dreaming... My body feels like a pine tree quivering in the wind.

FRIAR MARTIN: With these creaking tubs for vessels, it's a miracle we've arrived safe and sound. Thanks be to Our Lady of the Sea who has protected us.

JOANNA: If my mother were to hear you, with all the faith she has in this Armada that she thinks is invincible.

FRIAR MARTIN: If not invincible, at least miraculous!

SAILOR'S VOICE: Sand bars ahead!!

CAPTAIN'S VOICE: Hard to port! Bo'sun, look sharp!!

BOATSWAINS'S VOICE: Don't worry, cap'n! Everything's under control! I'll show these foreigners what a Spaniard can do!

(Loud grinding noise.)

CAPTAIN'S VOICE: Bo'sun! what the blazes are you doing?

BOATSWAIN'S VOICE: We've run aground, sir!

CAPTAIN'S VOICE: Damned fool!! This comes of not being on the look-out and wanting to show off with the whole of Europe watching us.

SAILOR'S VOICE: Leak in one of the holds!

CAPTAIN'S VOICE: Quick! Get the Princess into a dinghy!

SAILOR'S VOICE: The vessel carrying the royal luggage has run aground too!

FRIAR MARTIN: Your Highness, I think we're going to arrive minus your blankets.

JOANNA: Don't worry, Friar Martin, we'll cover ourselves over with tulips!

FRIAR MARTIN: Heaven help us! We're never going to get warm with all this fog!

(Sounds of popular celebration. The people have turned out into the streets, noisily welcoming the princess with shouts of "Long live Princess Joanna!")

PHILIP'S VOICE: Joanna! *(Pause.)* Joanna!! Joanna-a-a!!

JOANNA *(Confused)*: Philip? Is that you, my love? Where are you?

(Philip enters through the audience, running down the center aisle. He is a handsome, self-confident young man, not much older than Joanna.)

PHILIP: Joanna, my love! Joanna, my treasure! At last, the miracle has happened!

JOANNA: At last, I'm here at your side, for ever.

PHILIP: How long, how desperately I've been waiting for you!

JOANNA: Our life together will be far too short, Philip. Isn't it marvelous that the two of us have landed at the same moment, on the same shore?

PHILIP: Let me look at you. Oh, how lovely, how beautiful you are, Joanna.

JOANNA: Your eyes perform the miracle of making me lovely in your sight.

PHILIP: And you even speak French.

JOANNA: I learned it in secret with Friar Martin while we pretended to my governess that I was studying Latin.

PHILIP: On your lips, Joanna, French is as natural as a fish in water, as pollen in the air. It is like a tulip on your tongue.

JOANNA: Are you making fun of me when I've only just arrived?

PHILIP: On this day, sign language would be enough to seal this passion that I cannot hide.

JOANNA: Philip, we are still only betrothed. If these stormy winds were to carry our words to Castile, a special meeting of Parliament would be called to send me a spiritual director!

PHILIP: Forget about Castile! God is joy and goodness!

FRIAR MARTIN: Ahem! *(Pause.)* Your Highness?

PHILIP: Ah, who is this monk in his brown habit?

JOANNA: You haven't given me a chance to introduce him. This is Friar Martin; he is the one who taught me to read and write and to speak French. He also says that God is joy and goodness.

PHILIP: Then there are two of us, Joanna!

FRIAR MARTIN *(Pragmatically):* It would seem to me, if Your Highnesses will pardon me, that if things go on in this way, you should receive the sacrament of marriage as soon as possible. Sometimes love runs wild and it is not good to tether it. Even if it is wild, it is love after all.

JOANNA: I wonder what my ladies and gentlemen-in-waiting will say to that?

PHILIP: Let your strait-laced courtiers say what they will, since we are not going to have them in bed with us. Tomorrow we'll declare a holiday for them!

CISNEROS: Speaking of purely religious matters, the behavior of your daughter Joanna also leaves a lot to be desired...

ISABELLA: Obviously, Cisneros, today is one of those days when it would have been better never to have gotten out of bed!

CISNEROS: The moment she arrived in Flanders the marriage had to be hastily arranged, as it seems the Archduke was ready to take her there and then, without waiting for the blessing of the Church!

ISABELLA: With her consent?

CISNEROS: With her consent and with Friar Martin as witness!

ISABELLA: Whores there have always been, even in the best of families. Political necessity requires one to swallow many a bitter pill. What else?

CISNEROS: We already had information from our secret service about the depravity of customs and liturgy in the Flemish church, but the latest development is enough to infuriate God Himself!

ISABELLA: Have you spoken to Him?

CISNEROS: I have tried. Our clergy have unassailable proof of a new image of God which could do great harm to the consolidation of our Empire. The Flemish God is a permissive God who forgives.

ISABELLA: Can you be sure of that?

CISNEROS: This God, this new God whom your daughter Joanna has accepted, is a God who knows no revenge, a weak God who calls for total forgiveness, a God who radiates joy. War is becoming more necessary with every day that passes, Your Majesty.

ISABELLA: War is inevitable. As I say, some days it would be better not to get out of bed at all. *(Pause.)* Don Juan de Fonseca must be sent to Flanders. And we must put pressure on the secret service; we must infiltrate, infiltrate and destroy that false image of a forgiving God. Whatever is the world coming to? If God forgives every one, what are we supposed to be doing here? My daughter must be brought back to us, for we must never forget that my grandson Charles is the future Holy Roman Emperor. Have the secret agents redouble their efforts.

(The stage darkens. There is the sound of music and a baby crying. When the light comes up on JOANNA, she is rocking her baby daughter ISABELLA in a cradle. JOANNA looks very pale but very beautiful.)

JOANNA: Why are you crying, my love? You are going to be the sister of the most powerful man in the world, you know. Why these tears? Such beautiful eyes. Oh, now I see! You're soaking wet, my poor darling!

What am I going to do with you? Goodness knows what your grandmother will say when she sees you!

(Friar Martin, disguised as Moll Flanders, emerges from behind a curtain.)

FRIAR MARTIN: May I come in, Your Highness?

JOANNA: Goodness, Friar Martin! Why are you all dressed up like that? Is Carnival here already?

FRIAR MARTIN: I'm disguised as a rosy-cheeked dairy maid. The situation has become impossible, Your Highness. I've had to put up with a couple of country boys pinching my bottom before I could get through to reach you. And these lads certainly pinch hard! There was absolutely no other way to get in! As if we Spaniards had the plague!

JOANNA: Thank heaven I can talk to you in Spanish. What's the news from Spain?

FRIAR MARTIN *(Putting on a mock-serious face)*: Well, the news from Spain is the same as always. Don Juan de Fonseca and his crowd have everybody back there believing that this country is the anteroom to Hell, and the Queen is continually going to mass to pray for your soul. They've also spread the rumor that we dance our way through Mass here, and that you never go to confession and that, when you do receive communion, you nibble on the consecrated host and hop around in a frenzy!

JOANNA: Nothing surprises me! There are hidden interests at work to bring about my downfall. They'll stop at nothing to distort my behavior and discredit me. Whatever I do, I'm condemned for it. This is what I get for not giving in to them. I'm just not made of pliable metal, like gold, which adapts to any shape you impose on it. I am as I want to be, but love is not exactly a good language for making oneself understood. In Spain they say that I've gone crazy, but that's nothing new. They said it when I was a child because I used to ask questions about everything. And now they want to isolate me here, calling me a traitor when I take any initiative of my own. This is my punishment for loving my husband, painfully giving birth to children, and being loyal to my country.

FRIAR MARTIN: And where do I fit in, all dressed up like Moll Flanders?

JOANNA: I think the time has come to return to Spain and repair the damage that has been done.

FRIAR MARTIN: That would be madness, Your Highness. The latest news I have is that they're all in mourning. The Queen, your mother, has ordered everyone to wear black. I didn't dare tell you before, but...

JOANNA: Here we go again! What's the mystery now?

FRIAR MARTIN: Well, it seems that the Princess Margaret, you husband's sister, was too much for your brother John to handle and now he's as stiff as a leg of mutton!

JOANNA: Do you have to say it like that?

FRIAR MARTIN: To cut a long story short, Your Highness: The Duchess got him into bed the moment she arrived, and with that firm, rosy flesh of hers, all milk and honey, she had him gasping like a fish. Everybody at court tried to keep them apart, but the Queen intervened saying what God had joined together, let no one put asunder.

JOANNA: When the tragedy of death occurs and one is far away, it is usually sweetened by memories, but for your Joanna, this is the saddest of all days, because this unexpected end brings with it a much slower form of death for me. I'll have to assume the power of Castile, which is something I neither want nor ask. I know the people of my country and I wouldn't have the heart to be unjust, but power and justice rarely go together.

FRIAR MARTIN: No wonder Your Highness feels so sad, giving way to such pessimistic thoughts.

JOANNA: Some day, if I do ever come to power, I will give it all away to my people, and I will be the first to obey them.

FRIAR MARTIN: Hush, these walls have ears, Your Highness! There are more tattle-tales here than in a classful of first graders!

JOANNA: I begin to wonder whether the Archduke believes in me. I don't understand this silence. Perhaps he is keeping quiet about it so as not to make me suffer.

FRIAR MARTIN: You always have a kind word of forgiveness for him.

JOANNA: And if I don't forgive him, whom should I forgive? Life without him would be a wasteland for me! He opened my eyes to feelings I knew nothing at all about. He made me understand the quivering of my body. Without him I would understand nothing; with him I am both earth and furrow, the seed of autumn and the promise of spring. Apart from all that, I know he's a womanizer, but that is part of my lot as a woman.

FRIAR MARTIN: I can only listen in admiration!

PHILIP'S VOICE: Joanna, Joanna! Where is my love?

FRIAR MARTIN: Make the most of your chances, ma'am! Here he is, sounding for all the world like a nightingale! I have to admit that he's an attractive son-of-a-bitch.

JOANNA: Friar Martin!

FRIAR MARTIN: A slip of the tongue, Your Highness.

PHILIP: Look what I've brought you, Joanna. I picked them myself: tulips for my Queen!

JOANNA: And what is it that I have to forgive you for today?

PHILIP: Not being able to bring you the moon, Joanna.

JOANNA: But you know how angry your friends become when you pick tulips for the Spanish princess.

PHILIP: Why bother your head about such pettiness?

BROTHER MARTIN *(Sarcastically)*: Oh, why indeed?

PHILIP *(Noticing the rosy-faced 'girl' and showing annoyance)*: What? *(Pause.)* The only thing that matters is our happiness! Your health, your life, your smile I am here with you, aren't I? You will be the mother of many children, and there's nothing better for the pride and peace of a nation than to have a queen who gives birth regularly once a year!

JOANNA: Having the baby factory at home is good for national security, no doubt. That way, there's plenty of choice!

BROTHER MARTIN: Well said, Your Highness!

PHILIP: And who asked your opinion?

JOANNA: This morning I caught the nurse singing a lullaby to our little Charles and telling him that if he didn't go to sleep the Spanish armies would come and get him.

PHILIP *(Looking at Friar Martin and taking him to be the nurse)*: Is that what you said, you fat cow?

FRIAR MARTIN: Me? Why me? I'm not...

PHILIP: I'll whip your ass until it's as red as your face!

FRIAR MARTIN: But it wasn't me, Your Highness! It wasn't me! *(He exits hurriedly in a state of fright.)*

JOANNA: Ha, ha, ha!

PHILIP: What are you laughing at?

JOANNA: I have to laugh to keep from crying! Friar Martin had to disguise himself as a peasant woman because otherwise they wouldn't allow him into our apartments.

PHILIP: And you let him in? Don't you care what people may say?

JOANNA: Sometimes, Philip, I need to keep in touch with my Spanish friends. I can't believe that such a thing would mean the end of the world!

PHILIP: The time has come, Joanna, for me to tell you that I married *you*, not Spain.

JOANNA: But I don't have to stop being who I am simply because we are surrounded by a set of inept politicians! Neither Flanders nor Spain has the right to take away our happiness!

PHILIP *(He stops to consider this)*: Maybe you're right, Joanna, but the fact is that this is the way things have to be.

JOANNA: It's the way things have to be only because something is wrong, Philip!

PHILIP *(Realizing her argument is perfectly logical)*: All I know is that there isn't a single nook or cranny in the whole of this house where one can be alone, where one can be sure that one's words aren't being listened to back in Spain.

JOANNA: That's exactly what I'm saying, too!

PHILIP: It's not the same for you.

JOANNA: But it is! I feel the same as you do—harassed, spied on from all sides! They call you ambitious, but I am being called a whore and mentally deranged! Little by little I'm developing a complex about being unwanted, unwanted by you, unwanted by my father and mother, unwanted by anybody.

PHILIP *(Embracing her passionately)*: No, Joanna, no! Never that, my treasure, Joanna, my most beautiful beloved Joanna! You've put up for so long with all this stupidity and hostility, my love, and you never complain. But it's not my fault, Joanna! It's the fault of governments which have to defend their interests in this way.

JOANNA: Then let there be an end to governments.

PHILIP *(Covering her mouth with his hand, in fear of her being heard)*: Do you want to ruin us?

JOANNA: I don't want to be a puppet of the state, unless that means I can help the cause of justice, of peace and friendship between our countries. I don't want... I don't want... *(She suffers a kind of epileptic fit, shaking all over and sobbing.)*

PHILIP: Joanna, Joanna, you are too sensitive; you could never govern. But I love you just as you are, Joanna, and I would like to be like you, but if I were, we would be lost... I love you as you are, Joanna. We've made love so often in the light of dawn; we've watched the approach of dusk on so many evenings, hand in hand, building our dream-castles, that nothing should bother us, no matter who may be listening. You and I are like an impregnable cliff against which they will all be dashed and destroyed like flimsy ships in a storm.

JOANNA: You can't hide the truth from me, Philip. I'm nothing but an autumn leaf blown hither and thither by the wind.

PHILIP: I have a wonderful piece of news for you.

JOANNA: Another fairy tale?

PHILIP: This time it's true, Joanna.

JOANNA *(Wishing it might be true)*: Really?

PHILIP: Yes, Joanna. We're going to Spain! I have it all planned! *(He is lying)* I don't want your parents to think I'm holding you hostage...

JOANNA *(Like a child)*: Are you really going to take me to Spain?

PHILIP: That's what I've just said, Joanna.

JOANNA: Oh, how I love you, my darling! How happy my father and mother will be to see their grandchildren!

PHILIP: Well, the children will be staying here. It's a long journey and it is not a good idea.

JOANNA *(Reasonably)*: Of course, of course, I wasn't thinking.

PHILIP: Just close your eyes, and when you open them again, we'll be in Spain.

JOANNA *(Closing her eyes)*: Spain, Spain... Thank you, Philip. My heart is beating so fast with happiness that it's almost bursting!

PHILIP: We'll spend as little time as possible in France.

JOANNA: France, did you say? France? But France is at war with Spain!

PHILIP *(As always, he has a slick answer)*: Well, our visit will be a mere formality. We'll spend a few days with Louis, have a few drinks, attend a few balls, and be on our way.

JOANNA: And how do you expect me to turn up in Toledo after having had a few drinks with Louis XII? Sometimes you infuriate me, Philip! You never change! Let's go and have a few drinks in France! Don't you realize that my governess brought me up to believe that France was another name for Hell and that's where wicked children were sent to be punished?

PHILIP: Yes, and here we were taught something similar about the Spanish armies!

JOANNA: Well, that actually might be true.

PHILIP: In any case, I've already promised the French.

JOANNA: Is it too much to hope that you would ask me what I think?

PHILIP: I thought we might take a gift to your family to keep them happy—a religious painting, say of St. Joan of Arc, famous for her miracles, I believe.

JOANNA *(Almost with tears in her eyes)*: Oh, Philip, when will you understand that French saints are not exactly appreciated in Spain?

(Music. The lights go up on Queen Isabella and Cisneros.)

ISABELLA: Ave María Purísima!

CISNEROS: Blessed be Mary, conceived without sin.

ISABELLA: What news is there about Joanna?

CISNEROS: Your Majesty, we are most concerned.

ISABELLA: Surely one day you'll be able to offer me a piece of good news, Cardinal?

CISNEROS: I only wish I could, Your Majesty.

ISABELLA: Perhaps the world will come to an end tomorrow!

CISNEROS: How happy we would be.

ISABELLA: Let me hear the worst, Don Francisco.

CISNEROS: The Archduke Philip and the Princess Joanna have decided to take a vacation in France, with King Louis XII, on their way to Spain.

ISABELLA: I can't believe it!

CISNEROS: I said the very same thing when I found out through my secret service.

ISABELLA: When the King finds out about this—and we do, as we always say, reign as equals—he's going to bust his buttons if he hasn't already busted more powerful things!

CISNEROS: I've done what I could. I've even tried to perform a miracle.

ISABELLA: Nobody can beat the French and their tricks, not even saints like you, Cardinal.

CISNEROS: You know that I was able to make it rain all yesterday afternoon in Villaumbral.

ISABELLA: And you almost drowned the entire village!

CISNEROS: Not quite, Your Majesty, not quite.

ISABELLA: Well, I'll be writing to Rome about this latest miracle of yours, to inform our good friend Pope Leo X.

CISNEROS: May Heaven reward Your Majesty.

ISABELLA: Meanwhile, have preparations made to receive Princess Joanna and the confounded Archduke of Burgundy, may the devil take him! Arrange for colored lanterns and banners in the streets.

CISNEROS: But what about the period of mourning?

ISABELLA: It's to be relaxed for the time being.

CISNEROS: And what are we to do about the King's latest bastard?

ISABELLA: What do you expect? Include it in the official state budget, along with the rest of them.

(Organ music.)

(The people are in the streets welcoming JOANNA and PHILIP.)

OFFICIAL VOICE: Long live the King and Queen!

PEOPLE: Hurray!
OFFICIAL VOICE: Love live Isabella and Ferdinand!
PEOPLE: Hurray!
OFFICIAL VOICE: Long live the Archduke and Duchess of Burgundy!
PEOPLE: Hurray!
OFFICIAL VOICE: Long live Joanna of Castile!
PEOPLE: Hurray! ˙
OFFICIAL VOICE: Long live the Crown Princess of Castile!
PEOPLE: HURRAY!

(The organ music swells as CISNEROS appears in full pontifical vestments. JOANNA and PHILIP kneel as they are welcomed. QUEEN ISABELLA and KING FERDINAND stand a little apart and to one side.)

CISNEROS *(Conscious of his future role in history)*: Your Majesties, Your Highnesses, most dearly beloved in Christ. It is written in Holy Scripture and told by St. John in the Book of the Apocalypse, how the Lord God saved His people from Egypt and caused all disbelievers to perish; and how He keeps the fallen angels eternally imprisoned awaiting Judgment Day; and how Sodom and Gomorrah, and neighboring cities which had likewise fornicated and indulged in unnatural vices, were condemned to everlasting fire. In like manner, dearly beloved children, if we fail to follow the precepts of Holy Scripture under the divine mandate of our sovereigns Isabella and Ferdinand, the fire of Vulcan will fall upon Spain to purify her. And what do our sovereigns command? First, to love Spain, after God, above all things, not to betray her holy name and to pray to God for new saints in this land which has always been prodigal in wild thyme, lavender and saints.

PHILIP *(Aside, to Joanna)*: Joanna, my knees can't stand this much longer!

JOANNA: Hush!

CISNEROS *(Who has heard him)*: I have almost finished. Let us not wish for others what we would not wish for ourselves. Spain is great in her people, fragrant in her wines and boundless in her horizons. Let us rejoice therefore in Spain and in the future which Our Lord has reserved to her in history, under the rule of our Queen Isabella and our King Ferdinand,who, as we know, hold joint and equal sovereignty.

JOANNA *(Rushing to her mother's arms)*: Mother.

ISABELLA: Joanna.

JOANNA: Father.

FERDINAND: My dearest child.

JOANNA: Well, this is Philip.

PHILIP *(Kneeling and kissing the Queen's hand)*: Your Majesty.

ISABELLA: Rise, Philip, my son.

PHILIP *(As if he had rehearsed it all, kneeling to the King)*: Your Majesty.

FERDINAND: No need for such courtesy, Philip! No, it's not my wish to see you on your knees. Let me embrace you! The two of you are the future King and Queen of Spain now. The Queen and I feel deeply moved by the transcendence of this moment.

PHILIP: We too are moved and I, for my part, am pleasantly surprised. I can see this is a happy, lively court and that gives me great pleasure.

ISABELLA: Well, we do what we can, don't we, Your Grace?

CISNEROS *(Aside, to the Queen)*: What did you think of the colored lanterns?

ISABELLA: Very suitable.

JOANNA: We really have an awful image abroad. Nobody there ever mentions anything about us except the dreariness of our court with everyone always dressed in black.

FERDINAND: Your mother has lifted the rules on mourning.

ISABELLA: We've lightened up a lot lately! We're even going to introduce dancing classes as an educational requirement!

CISNEROS: The Pope will have to be informed about this, Your Majesty!

PHILIP *(Putting his foot in it)*: While we were in France, we were given these pictures. We thought you'd like them as a gift from us.

ISABELLA *(Scarcely able to hide her jealousy)*: Well, let's see! *(Changing her tone to speak to CISNEROS while FERDINAND engages PHILIP in conversation.)* Who is the silly girl in these pictures?

CISNEROS: The Maid of Orleans.

JOANNA: She is said to work many miracles.

ISABELLA: In my book a 'maid' is a virgin! How can she be a 'maid' if she's French?

FERDINAND: I was talking to Philip about the need for the two of them to go to Aragon and be presented to Parliament. If Spain is to be united within the multiplicity of her several nationalities...

ISABELLA: There is only one Spain: Castile.

FERDINAND: No, Isabella. Pardon me, but Spain is Castile and Aragon and Catalonia. Spain is a state made up of different nations, whether we like it or not.

ISABELLA: But Castile is still unique!

PHILIP: Quite honestly, it's all the same to me...

JOANNA: No, it's not the same, Philip, and the Netherlands are an excellent example of a state with different languages. You must forgive Philip, everyone. He's still a bit overwhelmed by being here. He feels nervous as he still doesn't understand our language very well.

PHILIP: I want to get to know this beautiful country: her people, her games, her dances... I want to dance a lot... Spain has very beautiful women with dark, handsome eyes...

ISABELLA *(To CISNEROS)*: We must stop this fellow right here and now, before he gets any further off track.

JOANNA *(Trying to excuse PHILIP)*: I've always talked to him about Spain with such love that he sees it all though the images I conjured up for him!

ISABELLA: That's all very well, my child, but he'll have to realize that this country isn't like France: it isn't a cabaret!

CISNEROS: Spain is beautiful because of her landscapes, fragrant on account of her wines, golden like the honey from the Alcarria hills and green like the emerald of her seas.

FERDINAND: And apart from all that, Philip, it is the country that you, in time, will be called upon to govern.

JOANNA: It's very important for you to listen to my father, Philip. He wants only the best for us.

PHILIP: The King of France also has some very good ideas about our future.

ISABELLA: Philip, you're a very charming young man and you've made a good impression here. We are happy to have you among us, and we'll do our best to ensure that there's plenty of dancing, if that's what concerns you. Cardinal Cisneros will take care of it all, but the music had better not be French!

FERDINAND: The first thing we must do is go to Aragon and have you recognized by Parliament as heirs to the throne.

ISABELLA: No! The first thing we must do is go to Mass and to confession. How long has it been, my child, since your last confession?

JOANNA: Well - um - I haven't been since I went abroad.

ISABELLA: My daughter is in a state of mortal sin and her father wants to rush her off to Aragon where they are all a bunch of atheists.

PHILIP: We brought our own cardinal with us—Cardinal Besacon.

ISABELLA: *Your* cardinal, my dear young man, is of no use here. Our cardinals are world-class, as you can see. After our cardinals come the ones from Aragon, perhaps, and then come all the rest. I can't imagine what your governess, Lady Beatrice, will say when she hears that you've both arrived here in a state of mortal sin!

CISNEROS: What am I to do about the dancing?

ISABELLA: Get Lady Beatrice working on it. Arrange for the Ladies' Group of Spanish Folk Dancers to put on a show out at one of the country castles.

(Music. JOANNA is combing her hair in front of a mirror. Enter FRIAR MARTIN.)

RIAR MARTIN: May I come in, Your Highness?

JOANNA: Yes, of course, Friar Martin.

FRIAR MARTIN: Your Highness, I'm mortified!

JOANNA: Oh dear, Friar Martin, you make my heart jump into my mouth! What has Philip been up to now?

FRIAR MARTIN: Well, Prince Philip is nowhere to be found.

JOANNA: Why is it that everyone wants me to go mad and die of jealousy?

FRIAR MARTIN: Do they?

JOANNA: Oh, if you only knew what's going on! I think they all get together to see who can invent the most outrageous story to tell me!

FRIAR MARTIN: As if they had nothing to hide about themselves!

JOANNA: Just what I was thinking! But I couldn't care less! So long as I see him happy and securely tucked into bed at night beside me.

FRIAR MARTIN: I think he is the happiest man in Castile today. And the Queen can't stand it!

JOANNA: They thought that Philip wanted to learn our regional folk dances! I've been laughing so much I nearly died. It's just too funny!

FRIAR MARTIN: And in full court dress too!

JOANNA: If it weren't all so ridiculous.

FRIAR MARTIN: Rumor has it that they're going to open up a high-class pub in Toledo for society parties and the like!

JOANNA: Philip must be behind that!

FRIAR MARTIN: The Cardinal is belching smoke from his ears, he's so mad!

JOANNA: And my mother's not far from it!

FRIAR MARTIN: The Queen's already saying that she'd almost prefer having the Moors back in Spain.

JOANNA: But the funniest thing is that since they threw out the Jews, there is no one to balance the accounts, and they've had to ask the Flemish flunkies for help! It's made them furious!

FRIAR MARTIN: You won't believe me, but I've seen the Duke of Alba himself adding up the cost of groceries on his fingers...

JOANNA: But you know, Friar Martin, that counting on your fingers is perfectly respectable. It shows you're an aristocrat.

FRIAR MARTIN: Your Highness, I feel so sorry for you.

JOANNA: You needn't! I'm very happy!

FRIAR MARTIN: You are the very stuff that happiness is made of!

JOANNA: And Philip's going to take part in a bullfight here in Toledo next Sunday.

FRIAR MARTIN: What a man! He seems to feel quite at home here now!

JOANNA: The person who doesn't feel at home at all is Cardinal Besacon. He's come down with tummy trouble after eating mushrooms.

FRIAR MARTIN: Maybe they were a gift to him from Cardinal Cisneros!

PHILIP'S VOICE: Joanna! Joanna!

FRIAR MARTIN: I must be going, Your Highness! Prince Philip sounds annoyed.

JOANNA: Well, you'll see how quickly I can calm him down.

(PHILIP rushes in like a hurricane.)

PHILIP: Joanna, I'm leaving! Pack my bags!

JOANNA: Whatever do you mean? You know how much you're looking forward to dazzling everyone with your performance at the bullfight.

PHILIP: I just can't take any more of this! I go to ten Masses a day, and it just isn't good for my health.

JOANNA: But you never stop, my love: games, tournaments, soirées ...

PHILIP: Cardinal Besacon has kicked the bucket!

JOANNA: I know. Too many mushrooms.

PHILIP: And who sent him the mushrooms, I would like to know?

JOANNA: Those mushrooms are delicious. Cardinal Cisneros gathers them personally, on his estate, especially for my mother.

PHILIP: Yes, but what if there was something else mixed in with the mushrooms.

JOANNA: What?

PHILIP: Maybe a poisonous fungus or two *(Pause.)* And maybe I'm next on the list! I'm going home, Joanna!

JOANNA: And what about me?

PHILIP: You're expecting again, so it would be foolhardy for you to...

JOANNA: So, *I'm* the one left behind to take care of the children!

PHILIP: Well, what do you expect? You're the one who keeps on having them!

JOANNA: Women are always the ones who have to suffer!

PHILIP: Do you think I'm to blame for that?

JOANNA: No, but you take advantage of it. I'm not a rabbit, Philip. What's more, you have no common sense. You behave as if we were tourists who've come down south from Flanders to enjoy the sun and music. Can't you get it into your head that we are heirs to the throne of Castile and Aragon?

PHILIP: Always supposing that your father doesn't remarry and have a son, and that we don't get separated.

JOANNA: All the more reason to make sure my father stays happy.

PHILIP: The only time your father's happy is when he is running after a wench. There's a joke going around, calling him the lace on a skirt because he's only happy when he's attached to one!

JOANNA: How vulgar can you get? But meanwhile, the precious Prince Philip will be off to see his friend, the King of France. Well, let me tell you, Philip, you are a dunce at politics. Your French friend is our greatest enemy! If you compromise with France, you compromise yourself and our very future. My mother's right. France can't be trusted, not even to go to Mass. They're our worst enemies and always will be. You don't have to be a genius to realize this. France will delight in seeing us go bankrupt, simply for geographical and political reasons. They'll do everything possible to divide us and, at the first opportunity, they'll stab us in the back. But if Spain is united to Flanders and to your father, the Emperor Maximilian, and if she is governed with an iron will, she will be a country full of hope for the future.

PHILIP: My dearest child, where on earth have you been keeping all that wisdom hidden?

JOANNA: It's not a matter of wisdom, Philip, but of reasoning.

PHILIP: You'll be hearing from me.

JOANNA: I refused to leave Flanders without you, and now you're going to leave me here alone?

PHILIP: It's only for a couple of months.

JOANNA: How long they'll be for me! Death would be better than this unexpected pain.

PHILIP: Goodbye.

JOANNA: Wait! If you go through that door, Philip, I want you to know that you'll be leaving behind you a cemetery where memories are buried, and a blinded she-wolf, a senseless betrayal. *(PHILIP exits.)* Philip, come back! Come ba-a-a-ck! *(The dying light accentuates her sobbing.)*

(On stage, ISABELLA and FERDINAND.)

FERDINAND: It's natural for her to want to be with her husband, Isabella.

ISABELLA: You call that clown a husband? If it hadn't been for me, I don't know what would have become of Spain.

FERDINAND: I don't understand why you blame me. Granted, Spain is indebted to you for contributing Castile to the union, but it is equally indebted to me for handing over Aragon.

ISABELLA: There's no comparison. Castile is rich; in Aragon, everybody's poor.

FERDINAND: Poor but honest.

ISABELLA: And they're always after the women.

FERDINAND: Isabella, just listen to yourself. You obviously have no respect for me at all.

ISABELLA: Can you imagine the cheek of it! A girl her age having the audacity to go on a hunger strike! And in the guard room of the castle, like a common prostitute waiting for nightfall! This daughter of ours, Ferdinand, is not quite right in the head.

FERDINAND: Do you really think so?

ISABELLA: What infuriates me most is that you take me for a fool. Do you think I'm not aware of the clause in your will regarding your daughter's accession to the throne of Aragon? You should be ashamed, at your age, of supposing you could outlive me and produce a son from a second marriage.

FERDINAND: Isabel, politics and patriotism sometimes outweigh personal feelings.

ISABELLA: Womanizer! Hypocrite! The palace is full of your bastards and you talk to me of feelings. Underneath all that fake respectability, there's a devil inside you.

FERDINAND: Come now, I won't mention your alleged levitations. They're nothing but the product of your concern over your daughter.

ISABELLA: And whom does she take after? Tell me that! Certainly not after me, nor anyone in my family.

FERDINAND: Nor in mine!

ISABELLA: So, not in your family, eh?

FERDINAND: We are first cousins, after all.

ISABELLA: In that case...

FERDINAND: Well, at least you recognize that.

ISABELLA: I think I'm not long for this world. Sometimes I look up to Heaven and I feel like screaming "Shit"!

FERDINAND: You frighten me, Isabella.

ISABELLA: This is what I get for wearing a crucifix round my neck all my life and for ridding the country of the Moors, down to the very last one of them!

FERDINAND: What are you complaining about? Our troops have just marched victoriously into Naples.

ISABELLA: I shall die when you need me most. Spain, without me, will fall apart.

FERDINAND: Unity must be preserved at all cost, even if it means riding over the corpses of the dead.

ISABELLA: You don't know what you're talking about... I'm alone, all alone!

FERDINAND: Isabella, you should go to confession! That is blasphemy!

ISABELLA: I feel the need to die, but before I do, I must talk to Joanna and convince her that she mustn't leave Spain. I'll be going to Medina immediately.

FERDINAND: The envoy from Philip will be here before you leave.

(Music. Spotlight on JOANNA, lying on a mattress, her face gaunt, her eyes staring blankly at nothing. FRIAR MARTIN is trying to get her to drink.)

FRIAR MARTIN: You must try to drink a little water, or at least moisten your lips. You haven't been up for a week. Come now, remember the rosy cheeks you had when you gave birth to the baby. When your mother sees you, she'll be worried to death.

JOANNA: And I'll be even closer to death if I have to remain here, separated from my husband and children.

FRIAR MARTIN: You've shown more patience than Job himself considering what you've suffered over that husband of yours.

JOANNA: Only those who have been wounded by the arrows of love can know its power and be overwhelmed by its sweetness.

FRIAR MARTIN: Oh, Your Highness, those arrows are poisoned! And they've left you with more holes than a colander!

JOANNA: I wouldn't have it otherwise, Friar Martin.

FRIAR MARTIN: The Queen is coming to visit you. If she sees you like this, she is going to get a fright.

JOANNA: My mother isn't frightened by anything any more, and the harm I do is only to myself, if this is harm. I refuse to be used ...

FRIAR MARTIN: Except by your husband?

JOANNA: I live and have my being in his love. He can do with me as he will.

FRIAR MARTIN: Now it's my turn to be scared. Either they ship you off to Flanders right now, or you will never move from here again.

JOANNA: I will not move for anything or anybody except to return to where I want to be.

FRIAR MARTIN: But, Your Highness, why stay here in the guard room?

JOANNA: The bigger the scandal, the better.

FRIAR MARTIN: God in Heaven, what strength of mind!

(Sound of trumpets.)

VOICE OFF: Captain of the guard! The cavalcade of Her Majesty, Queen Isabella of Castile, approaches! Guards, atte-e-e-n-tion!

OTHER VOICES: Guards, atte-e-e-n-tion! *(Echoing)* Atte-e-e-n-tion!

FRIAR MARTIN: Your Highness, aren't you shaking in your shoes?

JOANNA: I'm not shaking in the least. My pulse is steady.

FRIAR MARTIN: I envy you!

(The cavalcade appears. QUEEN ISABELLA dismounts.)

ISABELLA: No one is to approach within two hundred yards of the guard room.

FRIAR MARTIN *(Whispering to JOANNA)*: Take this wet handkerchief.

(A moment of silence.)

ISABELLA: Joanna, aren't you even going to get up to kiss your mother?

JOANNA: I can't, Mother. I haven't eaten anything for a week and my body won't respond, especially since the baby was born.

(At this point ISABELLA loses her patience and all sense of compassion.)

ISABELLA: What is this I hear? You are the daughter of the Queen of Castile! How can you possibly have been without food for a week?

JOANNA: And almost without water.

ISABELLA: Are you determined to destroy the good name of Castile?

JOANNA: No, Mother. I simply want you to allow me to return to Philip and my children.

ISABELLA: You want to return to that irresponsible, heartless, dandified fool?

JOANNA: I want to be with my husband, with the man I love.

ISABELLA: You want me to believe that *this* is love? Who can be responsible for your turning out like this? You are just like him - -you've sunken to the lowest of the low. Can't you see yourself lying there on that mattress, like any common slut? Only a whore does what you are doing.

JOANNA: Why don't you speak the truth instead of searching for excuses, which I understand, because I am a mother too, but that's not the point. You're losing your greatest virtue, which is to call a spade a spade. The truth is that reasons of state oblige you to keep me here.

ISABELLA: If you understand so well, why do you insist on making us go through all this?

JOANNA: Why do I have to be the one who... ?

ISABELLA: Because you are Spanish.

JOANNA: I no longer know what I am, Mother.

ISABELLA: You are Spanish whether you like it or not. The trouble is that you are insane... insane!

JOANNA: I want to be true to my destiny even though I realize that destiny isn't my friend just now. But time, which is my greatest ally, will defend me. I know that this is but the beginning of a difficult road, and that I'm doomed, but I shall go on, because I gave my promise to this man..

ISABELLA: A man who has enslaved you to his lust, getting you perpetually pregnant like a rabbit.

JOANNA: I would rather that than have to warehouse his bastards in the garrets of a castle!

ISABELLA: How dare you say that to your mother?

JOANNA: I say it to the Queen of Castile.

ISABELLA *(Raising her hand)*: Say it again, if you dare!

JOANNA: I say it to the Queen of Spain!

(ISABELLA slaps JOANNA.)

ISABELLA: Joanna, oh my child, forgive me! Dearest little rebel! Always taking me to task! My angel, my little rebel!

JOANNA: That's what you always used to call me when I was a child.

ISABELLA *(Caressing her)*: My own darling! Why did I ever let you go away to that strange country?

JOANNA: In that strange country, in spite of everything, I was the happiest woman in the world and I produced a future emperor for Spain!

ISABELLA: Let's not talk about that now. Let me hug you. I've left a red mark on your face! And to think that we let down the traditional dignity of our court with all that dancing just to please that wild husband of yours. We even put up colored lanterns in his honor!

JOANNA: But now you've put the court back in black!

ISABELLA *(Reverting to being Queen)*: Spain is a nation, not a circus! The last thing I want is for Spain to become a satellite of France and Maximilian. Fortunately I will die before that happens.

JOANNA: Don't think about such things now!

ISABELLA: Joanna, you've won, for today. But don't ever do this to me again. Look, I've brought you some candy. We can't have that devil see you looking so gaunt and thin.

JOANNA *(Her face lights up.)*: Then you'll let me go?

ISABELLA: Philip has sent for you. He wants you there with him. Oh, if only it were for love of you.

JOANNA: It is, Mother!

ISABELLA: I doubt it, my child, but if that's what you want, so be it. There's only one thing I ask of you.

JOANNA: Granted!

ISABELLA: Don't go by way of France!

JOANNA: But what if Philip is offended?

ISABELLA: You have promised me, and it's the last thing I ask of you before I die.

JOANNA *(With tears in her eyes)*: Mother...

ISABELLA: The Admiral will take you on board at Laredo.

JOANNA: Mother... what a beautiful mother you are.

ISABELLA: And you, Joanna, are my beautiful love. Now get along with you, before I change my mind. I hate to think of that thief stealing my daughter away again!

JOANNA: Don't worry about it any more!

END OF PART ONE

PART TWO

JOANNA of Castile returns to the Netherlands. This scene is a repetition of the one in which she first set sail to meet Philip. When the action begins, JOANNA is standing in the prow of the ship with FRIAR MARTIN by her side. Daybreak, with fog. A kind of groaning can be heard from time to time: it is the ship complaining of the pain in its nautical belly as the seas beat against its ribs.

CAPTAIN'S VOICE: Anything to report?

LOOKOUT'S VOICE: Nothing, sir.

CAPTAIN'S VOICE: Bo'sun!

BOATSWAIN'S VOICE: Sir?

CAPTAIN'S VOICE: Maintain full alert!

BOATSWAIN'S VOICE: Don't worry, sir! Making harbor this time will be like floating in on silk!

JOANNA: Oh, Friar Martin, my heart's in my mouth and there are shivers running up and down my spine!

FRIAR MARTIN: You sound like a young bride again....

JOANNA: I still feel like a bride, about to relive that first unforgettable night,

FRIAR MARTIN: So, what your royal mother sometimes says really is true: it's an ill wind that blows nobody any good!

JOANNA: That's the destiny of people like me who believe that happiness isn't a perennial flower but an ephemeral and unexpected gift.

LOOKOUT'S VOICE: Land ho! *(Slowly, with the dawn, the fog begins to lift.)*

CAPTAIN'S VOICE: D'you hear that, Bo'sun?

BOATSWAIN'S VOICE: I heard it, Cap'n, and by heaven, we'll be the admiration of the whole of Europe this time!

(Dull grating noise.)

APTAIN'S VOICE *(Furious)*: What the hell is going on, bo'sun?

BOATSWAIN'S VOICE: We've run aground again, sir!

CAPTAIN'S VOICE: Then be prepared to memorize the catechism and write out "I am a donkey" two hundred times! Come on now, look sharp! Launch a dinghy for the princess and her people!

FRIAR MARTIN: It's a good thing we don't have to worry about blankets this time, ma'am.

JOANNA: I have no need of them now. I've enough with Philip's arms to keep me warm.

FRIAR MARTIN: You're lucky to have that to look forward to; you can almost enjoy getting stuck on a sandbank!

JOANNA *(Laughing happily)*: Ha, ha, ha ...

(Change of scene and lighting. JOANNA rushes, like a young girl, into the arms of Philip, who is waiting for her.)

JOANNA: Philip! Philip! *(Falling into his arms.)* Philip, my love, together again!

PHILIP *(Greeting her coldly)*: Hello, Joanna. How are you? It's nice to see you again.

JOANNA: Only 'nice' to see me? Haven't you been counting the days, the hours, the minutes? Hasn't it seemed that they would never pass? I thought that time had stood still just to punish me!

PHILIP *(His tone is still cold)*: You don't look like yourself.

JOANNA *(Somewhat taken aback)*: Surely you've been told that we've had another son and he's been named Ferdinand, like my father.

PHILIP: I've been so busy I haven't even had time to pick a few tulips for you.

JOANNA: A good thing you didn't! You were always getting into trouble for that! Look! This is our son Ferdinand. He slept through the entire journey! See? He has your eyes, and the Habsburg fingers.

PHILIP *(Going through the motions like a dutiful husband)*: Did the baby come on time? Did everything proceed normally?

JOANNA: The baby came out backwards like everything else that happens to me—feet first!

PHILIP: I didn't hear a single word from you.

JOANNA: There was no way of reaching you. You must have been terribly busy. Anyway, you know the situation you left me in.

PHILIP: Europe is going through a sensitive crisis and we must lay the foundations for the future of society.

JOANNA: Surely, one day, after all you've put into it, you'll get what you want.

PHILIP: Well... you can't imagine how happy I am to see you.

JOANNA: Are you sure?

PHILIP: Your new apartments have been prepared for you.

JOANNA: What do you mean—'new' apartments?

(Sounds of loud feminine laughter.)

FEMALE VOICE: Philippe! Philippe! Tu vas venir? Je t'attends!

JOANNA: Oh, I see! You've been making a pair of horns for me!

PHILIP: I've what?

JOANNA: That's a common Spanish expression.

PHILIP: Well, it's not the proper expression, at least not here in Flanders!

JOANNA: In Spain maybe we don't go far enough, but here you go too far. Who is there in my rooms? I want an answer—now!

PHILIP *(Suddenly trying to be affectionate)*: Surely you're not jealous, Joanna?

JOANNA: Don't touch me! I'm going to find out what's going on right now! Whoever she is, she's going to pay dearly for it! Here! *(She hands him the baby wrapped in its blanket.)* He's yours!

PHILIP: Joanna, come back! You must be imagining you heard voices! Friar Martin, did *you* hear anything?

FRIAR MARTIN: Me? Nothing. And if I did, I'd keep mum about it.

PHILIP *(Annoyed with FRIAR MARTIN)*: In this place, nobody hears anything except what I say they hear!

FRIAR MARTIN: Just what I was about to say myself.

JOANNA'S VOICE: Qui êtes-vous? Sortez immédiatement de cette pièce!

FEMALE VOICE: Moi? *(Frightened.)* Philippe! Viens!

JOANNA'S VOICE: Sortez ou vous aurez affaire a moi!

FEMALE VOICE: A-a-ah mes cheveux! Au secours, à moi, Philippe!

JOANNA'S VOICE: Sortez! Sortez! Sortez!

(Screams and cries of 'ouch,' turning into a phenomenal row, punctuated by an occasional expletive in Spanish such as 'bitch' etc. Philip and Friar Martin are speechless. Joanna enters carrying scissors and a lock of hair.)

JOANNA: Here! This bitch's hair is for you!

PHILIP *(Seeing his opportunity)*: No one behaves as you have done except somebody who is thoroughly spiteful and mentally unhinged! Yes, you're insane, totally insane!

JOANNA: In Spain we'd say that you've been cheating on me and I'll not stand for it! Is this what I've broken all my family ties for? You son-of-a-bitch! Have you no shame? I've given you all I have: my body, my soul and even my country! I've held nothing back. And you didn't even have the decency to hide it from me! Instead, you taunted me in the meanest, most contemptible way! Why, oh why did I have to fall in love with you?

PHILIP: You're overwrought, Joanna. Throw those scissors on the floor!

JOANNA: So you still expect me to obey you, do you? You know what you are? A little shit who keeps the marital bed warm with a bunny-rabbit from the wood-pile! You're a fortune-hunter, a flunkey!

PHILIP: Take care what you say, Joanna, and remember who you are!

JOANNA: I'm heir to the throne of Castile, the richest nation in Europe!

PHILIP: Careful now!

JOANNA: And you are a flunkey, a flunkey of the French king! *(PHILIP slaps JOANNA on the face.)* So! You hit me! Now I understand! I was expecting you to kiss me and then to forgive you for everything, but instead you slap me in the face!

PHILIP *(To FRIAR MARTIN)*: You see, Friar Martin! You are a witness. The Princess is mentally deranged.

JOANNA: Get out! Get away from me! I never want to see you again! You've betrayed me. Your love is nothing but a bag of trash full of vile ambitions! As far as I'm concerned, you are dead, Philip, dead from now on!*(She falls to the ground, sobbing.)*

(Change of scene and lighting. Sounds of a choir of monks singing in the Benedictine Abbey of St.Martin. ISABELLA is lying in bed, CISNEROS in attendance.)

ISNEROS: How is Your Majesty feeling?

ISABELLA: Not well, not well at all. This is the end.

CISNEROS: Nobody is going to believe that. Look at those cheeks, fresh as a russet apple, that God has blessed you with this morning!

ISABELLA: The worm of death is hidden within the apple. What news do you bring?

CISNEROS: Good news, Your Majesty.

ISABELLA: In that case you must think me very sick indeed.

CISNEROS: No fear of that! This will make you feel much happier. Our conversion business in Granada is going full steam ahead. There are already more than twenty thousand who have accepted the faith.

ISABELLA: Not bad, not bad.

CISNEROS: In a single confiscation ceremony, we have burned more than twelve thousand copies of the Koran. The Grand Inquisitor Torquemada is doing great work for Christendom. It's a joy to watch the man burning the Koran!

ISABELLA: Obviously, I must be about to die and you wish to see me happy on my final journey.

CISNEROS: There are some days, Your Majesty, that give one reason to smile, although we, as Spaniards, with the rest of Christendom can never rest until Oran falls to Christian forces.

ISABELLA: I know that victory will be yours one day, but I will have to celebrate it at the right hand of God the Father, surrounded by the angels, archangels, cherubim and thrones...

CISNEROS *(Cutting in)*: And what news is there from the Pope? Saint Isidrus was declared a saint simply because the angels came down to help him plough the earth!

ISABELLA: Impatience never was the stuff that saints are made of. The Pope is apprised of your talents and he has sent me a letter requiring you to decrease the number of your days of fasting and abstinence. No one can fight the infidel if his body is weak and skinny.

CISNEROS *(Like a child)*: You mean the Pope knows all about me?

ISABELLA: He's called infallible for good reason. Sometimes you seem to have doubts...

CISNEROS: When I'm a saint, I'll perform a miracle every day for Spain.

ISABELLA *(Showing signs of being in pain)*: We're certainly going to need them to bring this country into line, with all these self-taught geniuses, some of them as stubborn as mules.

CISNEROS: Here comes His Majesty.

ISABELLA: I'm afraid he's here to ask for something. He always does.

CISNEROS: He is the King.

ISABELLA: But he is also a man. Why can't I be allowed to die in peace?

(Enter FERDINAND.)

FERDINAND: Isabella, Isabella, I have some bad news.

ISABELLA: Aren't you going to ask me how I am?

FERDINAND *(Solicitous)*: How are you? How are you, Isabella?

ISABELLA: How do you think I am? I'm dying, of course.

FERDINAND: Don't say things like that, Isabella. You will never die! You'll leave a mark that can never be erased.

ISABELLA: Exaggeration doesn't become you, Ferdinand, nor your better-than-usual flattery, now that we stand in the presence of the Great Enemy.

FERDINAND: This is very important, Isabella, and very frightening.

CISNEROS: It's a good thing I'm not the only one to bring bad news.

ISABELLA: In your case, you should either bring good news or stop performing portentous miracles. *(CISNEROS is put out.)*

FERDINAND: This is truly terrifying, Isabella. Our son-in-law Philip has sent us a diary in which Friar Martin has been keeping notes, describing the behavior of our daughter since she returned to Flanders. It's enough to bring tears to your eyes. *(But they don't come to his.)* Joanna, our daughter has gone insane. She has completely lost her mind and has had to be confined, after she cut off the hair of one of the ladies of the court in a fit of frenzy. Joanna is mad, irreversibly mad!

CISNEROS: What a disgrace for Spain!

FERDINAND: And now we'll all be judged to be like her!

(Isabella, deeply affected, turns her head away and weeps.)

FERDINAND: Isabella, Isabella, I didn't want to tell you ... but we have a responsibility to Spain.

ISABELLA: My poor Joanna! My poor little rebel! So that's how he returned your love! My own little girl...

FERDINAND: Are you going to make excuses for her?

ISABELLA: I'm not excusing her. I'm only reproaching myself for having let her leave, for having allowed this marriage. When I did that, I obviously made the biggest political mistake of my life.

CISNEROS: The court of Flanders, riddled with Erasmian notions, is to blame for the softening of her brain.

FERDINAND *(Adding more fuel to the flames)*: If only we had known about all that beforehand.

CISNEROS: Things have degenerated so badly over there that they even praise madness nowadays in some of the more perverse of their modern plays!

ISABELLA: Go on, go on, make me feel even worse!

FERDINAND: This is not the worst!

(CISNEROS and ISABELLA react sharply.)

ISABELLA: More madness, Ferdinand?

CISNEROS: This evening I'll have to perform a miracle!

FERDINAND: The worst of all is that our son-in-law, that whey-faced ninny, has joined the French and Maximilian in declaring that I'm no longer considered to be King of Spain, only of Aragon! *(He falls disconsolately at the foot of ISABELLA'S bed.)*

ISABELLA: But our daughter will still be Queen, won't she?

FERDINAND: Yes, but *I'm* not to be King! I'm being ostracized!

ISABELLA: Well, the important thing is that the whole country should be united under Joanna.

FERDINAND: H'm. That young Philip has the instincts of a bloodhound.

CISNEROS *(Maliciously)*: Where would Aragon be without the grain and the wealth of Castile?

ISABELLA: All comparisons are odious.

FERDINAND: You can't go and leave me alone now, Isabella.

ISABELLA: Oh, Ferdinand, Ferdinand. *(To CISNEROS.)* Be so kind as to go and bring the Notary General of the Kingdom to us, Cardinal.

CISNEROS: As Your Majesty commands. *(He goes out, winking an eye at FERDINAND.)*

ISABELLA: Come here, Ferdinand. I sent Cisneros on an errand because I don't want him to hear what I have to tell you. *(CISNEROS is listening behind a curtain.)* You don't deserve what I'm about to do for you, Ferdinand. I know I'm dying; these are my last hours, but this is not the time for reproaches, nor for silence. We have fought together for Spain, though from different viewpoints. Yes, you've been faithful to me politically, but how distant you've always been from me in your heart! Now that I'm about to die and nobody can hear us, I'll tell you this: Ferdinand, you've always been a playboy! Whatever history may say, you are a playboy—the playboy of Aragon!

FERDINAND: That's not true, Isabella, it's not true. I've never been an adulterer in my heart.

ISABELLA: But you have with every other part of you!

(Enter CISNEROS.)

CISNEROS: Ahem! The Notary General is here.

ISABELLA: I no longer need him. Bring me a pen, ink and paper!

FERDINAND: Shall I dictate to you?

ISABELLA: That won't be necessary. *(She takes up the pen and paper.)* "On this date, the twenty-third of November, fifteen hundred and four, I, Isabella of Castile, Queen of Spain by the Grace of God, do hereby ordain that, in the event of my dearly-beloved daughter Joanna being unable or unwilling to perform the duties of government, Ferdinand, my husband, King of Aragon, shall reign, govern and administer the realm in her name."

(Music. ISABELLA, with tears in her eyes, sadly turns her head away.)

FERDINAND: God bless you, Isabella! And may I answer to Him if I ever fail to govern faithfully.

CISNEROS: What a noble soul!

FERDINAND *(Taking CISNEROS aside)*: Cancel the prayers for her recovery in all the churches of the realm and have them replaced with prayers for the salvation of her soul.

(Music. Slow change of scene. As the lighting gradually returns, the silence is shattered by the sounds of keys and the closing of iron doors. JOANNA OF CASTILE is lying on the floor. She is no longer a young and attractive girl but a woman broken by suffering. She gazes around. Her eyes are reddened and her attire is different. Once more, we can hear the sounds of a key turning and the same reverberations of prison doors, and then footsteps. LUIS FERRER emerges from the shadows. He is the man charged by FERDINAND THE CATHOLIC to keep watch over his daughter in the castle of Tordesillas. This character is played by the same actor who played FRIAR MARTIN.)

JOANNA: Friar Martin, is that you? Have you come to set me free? How strange you look! Why are you dressed like that? Where am I?

LUIS FERRER: Don't excite yourself, my lady. You are here in the castle at Tordesillas, and I am Luis Ferrer, sent by your father to look after you.

JOANNA: You look like Friar Martin.

LUIS FERRER: Friar Martin committed suicide when he came back here to Spain. He hanged himself in Burgos.

JOANNA: And why was I never informed? *(Then, as if she were speaking to Friar Martin.)* Why did you do that? What did they do to you?

LUIS FERRER: They say he was used by your husband Philip to discredit you as Queen of Castile.

JOANNA: That can't be true. Friar Martin was loyal to me. Nobody knew better than he did what I suffered in Flanders. *(Hallucinating.)* Is it true, Friar Martin? Were you the one who betrayed me like a common Judas? Friar Martin, speak to me!

LUIS FERRER: Calm down, Your Highness. It's all over now and you are well protected, in good hands.

JOANNA: I don't need your protection. I am the Queen of Castile, and the Queen is protected by whomever she chooses. *(Hallucinating, in a tender voice.)* You, was it you who betrayed me to my mother?

LUIS FERRER: Your Highness, you are overexcited.

JOANNA: No, no, don't come any closer. I can see who you are. You are Friar Martin. I see it all. You sent them the story of my madness. Well done, Friar Martin! How generous of you! And what was the reward they gave you when you came back to Spain? A sorry rope to hang yourself with! Was that the payment? Is it so wrong to love? Of course, if I had been worldly-wise, selfish and ambitious, none of this would have happened. We would all have been perfectly respectable. But I had to feel what it was to love. To love everyone. And I had to put up with his sleeping around, pinching the buttocks of all the ladies-in-waiting before my very eyes, and on top of everything else, I had to pretend I didn't care! Then you go and write to my parents saying that I've gone mad, that I've caused a scandal in a foreign court where the honor of the Catholic Monarchs is at stake... Mother, Mother, is there any truth in all these intrigues?

(QUEEN ISABELLA appears for a while out of the shadows.)

ISABELLA: Oh Joanna, Joanna. Every time I look at you I see the face of your grandmother.

JOANNA *(Dreaming)*: Mommy, Mommy, whom will I marry?

ISABELLA: The most important man in the world, because you are going to be Queen of an empire greater than anyone has ever known! But your father must be kept on a tight rein. He's a good man but he's very ambitious... and irresponsible too!

JOANNA: Then I'm going to be a queen ... a queen!

ISABELLA: Though I fear you have a heart that's too big for a queen....

JOANNA: Big enough to love you all when I'm in power!

ISABELLA: Joanna, my love, my dearest little rebel! *(She disappears.)*

JOANNA: Mommy, don't go! Tell me everything, Mommy! Mommy! *(Pause.)* Mother!

LUIS FERRER: Why inflict more suffering on us all? It's all over, Your Highness. You can be happy now, here in Tordesillas, knowing that your father governs for you in Castile and that his armies are winning in Italy!

JOANNA: Nobody knows better than I do what my father's doing. *(Moving away to stand alone.)* And on top of everything, that son-of-a-bitch went off leaving me pregnant, as men always do.

LUIS FERRER: The baby princess Katherine is getting big enough now to play hopscotch!

JOANNA: What does that matter to you? *(She kneels down as if she were playing on the floor.)* Philip used to settle everything in bed. You liar, you won me over every night, persuading me to say yes to everything.

PHILIP'S VOICE: Joanna! Joanna!

JOANNA *(Her eyes light up)*: Philip, Philip, where are you?

(PHILIP, very sure of himself, enters, carrying a piece of paper.)

PHILIP: I won't put up with this Archbishop a minute longer. He's after me all the time, as if I were his altar boy! It's "Prince Philip this" and "Prince Philip that" the whole time. I'm sick of so much "Prince Philip." He's going to wear out my name! And he goes on and on about my not going to confession at Easter...

JOANNA: Doesn't he realize that you're a permanent Easter gift yourself?

PHILIP: What do you mean by that?

JOANNA: I mean that where you are, Spring is never far behind!

PHILIP: What are you getting at?

JOANNA: Never mind now...

PHILIP: Don't you see that we non-Spaniards, the avant-garde ...

JOANNA: Don't get too full of yourself or I'll have you sent to Salamanca, like the Marquis of Villena.

PHILIP: And what has the Marquis done now?

JOANNA: He's been kicking out like a mule, which is about all he knows how to do. These aristocrats will have to be sent to school, or to the vet.

PHILIP: In Europe things are different.

JOANNA: Perhaps people there are not so uncouth; perhaps they're as smooth as silk, but they've always got their eye on the bottom line. They'd kill their own father to make a profit!

PHILIP: My men are all fine gentlemen!

JOANNA: D'you know what my priceless mother would've said to that? She would've told you that all fine gentlemen are ass-holes. We can't discriminate, Philip. In this court—Heaven help us!—the goats are mixed in with the sheep. Where else but in this country does everyone talk about everything except what's important—like jobs, and justice? It's high time for us to take charge!

PHILIP: You have some very strange ideas about how to govern a nation.

JOANNA: Wealth can't be drawn on paper, Philip: it has to be created, but not by exploiting the weakest! Spain is like an uncut diamond. and we are the jewel cutters. But my father is determined to act like a butcher of sheep and goats.

PHILIP: Your father fleeces us with his taxes.

JOANNA: And if it were up to you, what would you do? Oh, you adore money too.

PHILIP: Well, really, I...

JOANNA: It's all quite simple. If we are the sovereigns, let's take the government into our hands.

PHILIP: But your father won't let us. He's the dog in the manger!

JOANNA: My mother is the one who has left us our true legacy: our place in history. Let's make sure that our children understand it. History should remember her as a woman whose aim was not to create a nation by brute force but to fashion a single state while respecting the uniqueness of each of its kingdoms, making fundamental laws for all, but then allowing the kingdoms to govern themselves as each saw fit.

PHILIP *(Not understanding or caring in the least)*: Oh, that's a great idea! *(Coming to what really interests him.)* But I'm not willing to let your father keep all the money. The income from Castile is...

JOANNA: To help make Spain more beautiful!

PHILIP: And to help pay my debts! We can't let your father control the nation's historic treasure.

JOANNA: Let's go out and talk to the people. Let's ask them about their needs and then see justice done. Let's patronize the sciences and encourage the search for wisdom. If we do this everything else will fall into place.

PHILIP: You're crazy, Joanna. Go out and talk to the people? You mean, give them a chance to kill us? The idea is preposterous! A queen talking to her people? In any case, the people never understand anything! They misinterpret things or give them double meanings. *(He starts to fondle her.)* You're so naive!

JOANNA: Don't! I'm not in the mood for games! I'm very angry with you.

PHILIP: You know what? I'm going to take you to the bullfight in Valladolid.

JOANNA: I don't feel like bullfights! Philip, no! Not here! You're like a rooster with a broody hen... It doesn't mean a thing to you.

PHILIP: Don't you feel the desire for ...

JOANNA: No!

PHILIP: I ought to give you a good thrashing.

(They indulge in playing the game of love, falling on the floor and rolling over and over, laughing.)

JOANNA: You always know how to get around me. You know that I don't have the strength to resist, that I'm weak in body and spirit. You wouldn't be setting me up again for another of your little adventures, would you?

PHILIP: Oh, Joanna, you fill me with radiance and with sadness. I need you too, Joanna; I need your beautiful love. *(Then, as if the matter were of no importance.)* Look, I've brought this order for you to sign. I need four hundred thousand ducats to pay the German troops who escorted us here. Your father has left us without a dime.

JOANNA: Why do you come and ask me when you know full well that I count for nothing any more around here?

PHILIP: Whom should I go to then?

JOANNA: Anyone but me. Go and pick someone else's pockets! *(She gives in and signs.)* And now you're going? Leaving me with the honey on my lips?

PHILIP: This is an urgent business matter, Joanna. The troops are threatening to riot. You must understand...

JOANNA: At least, leave me pregnant! That's my job, isn't it?

PHILIP: Don't be such a nag, Joanna! I'll be back and we'll make love then.

JOANNA: When you come back, I shall be dead!

PHILIP: You love to exaggerate, don't you?

JOANNA: I loathe being a woman! Love for us means having to humiliate ourselves, opening up our legs.

PHILIP: You are so Spanish, Joanna, always dramatizing everything. Look how good you are at crochet and embroidery. *PHILIP exits laughing, leaving her alone.)*

JOANNA: How quickly you've picked up on our Spanish ways, and turned them to your advantage. *(JOANNA exits after PHILIP and can now be seen again as a prisoner. We hear the sound of iron gates clanging shut, one after another.)* Damn you! Damn you! You got what you wanted and now you have no need of me. *(The blood rushes to her head.)* Philip, you son-of-a-bitch! May your mother rot in hell! This is the last trick you'll ever play on me! Who do you think you are, you puppet prince, you whey-faced monkey! Don't ever come here again with your tulips! Never talk to me again about the beautiful love of Joanna, because it's no longer true. No, it's no longer true. And all because I've been weak and forgiving. From now on, you're all going to see the devil inside me! And I shall be Joanna, yes, Joanna of Castile, for that's who I really am. Up to now, you've all taken advantage of my love, but now, be warned! The party's over! For the sake of love, I've betrayed my lineage and my country. *(She sobs.)* I didn't cry when I came into the world: I smiled lovingly at my mother! I've given my blood and turned it into ripe cherries. I've made springtime out of my darkness and oceans out of my tears and now you keep me here in solitary confinement, hostage to your worldly ambitions.

(Music. Enter LUIS FERRER.)

LUIS FERRER: Why don't you rest, Your Highness?

JOANNA: And who are you to tell me to rest? A queen doesn't need to rest, unless she's lame. Does Your Excellency know what it is to be lame? I don't need support from anyone, least of all from a jailer.

LUIS FERRER: You are torturing yourself for no reason.

JOANNA: I prefer to torture myself with hope rather than be tortured by hatred and solitude. Is it torture to love Spain? No, it's only madness.

LUIS FERRER: You should be glad to know that your father reigns in your stead so that you can be free to love in comfort.

JOANNA: My only comfort will come with death. Open up the gates of this castle and let me kiss the sun of Castile.

LUIS FERRER: Where can you be better off than by the side of your daughter Katherine?

JOANNA: My little girl is always gazing out of the window. My prison is her prison, too. A tiny snowflake fallen among the shadows.

LUIS FERRER: Your father has given orders that you should lack for nothing. Your life is precious to Castile.

JOANNA: My life may be precious to my father; it's not to me. Although he would not have me be queen, he would not have me die. As for me, the only thing I prize is freedom. And yet I must be thankful that they haven't needed me to die, for if that were so, dead I would surely be. No one will ever know what goes on in the dark corridors of power.

LUIS FERRER: You never give thanks to God. God is not here with you.

JOANNA: God is here only in happiness and I'm not happy, nor do I wish to be.

LUIS FERRER: Clearly they were right to shut you away.

JOANNA: What do you expect of me? To be happy when I'm shut away? God can't be with me when I'm always weeping. Let others enjoy His company.

LUIS FERRER: I've brought you something to eat.

JOANNA: You're wasting your time, Ferrer. I'm not opening my mouth! I won't give you the pleasure of telling my father that I'm putting on weight.

LUIS FERRER: It saddens your father to hear that you're not eating.

JOANNA: Is he really so concerned about me?

LUIS FERRER: You haven't eaten anything for six days and I am held responsible.

JOANNA: It's funny to see you so put out.

LUIS FERRER: I may have to take more drastic measures. I'm only doing my duty.

JOANNA: How true it is, Ferrer, that there are many times when people can't feel very proud of doing what is called their duty.

LUIS FERRER: My honor is at stake.

JOANNA: Honor, too, is often an embarrassment.

LUIS FERRER: Your Highness, this can't go on. You can't be allowed to go on taunting me. You are possessed by the devil! God has abandoned you! Curse you for a madwoman!

(FERRER rushes upon JOANNA, and there is a struggle. She almost falls into the arms of her jailer.)

LUIS FERRER: You can be thankful that you're the daughter of my lord the King; if not...

JOANNA: What are you waiting for? Aren't you going to rape me, jailer? *(He twists her arm.)* A-a-ah... *(He tortures her by tying her hands to the back of a chair.)* A-a-ah ...

LUIS FERRER: Now you won't be so quick with your answers. So! You want to be queen, do you? Many women would give anything to be in your shoes. *(When FERRER looks away, JOANNA bites him)* A-a-ah! You damned viper! Bite me, would you? Kind words don't work with you, do they?

(In a fit of rage, FERRER hits her repeatedly.)

JOANNA: Oh...oh...oh...Untie me, untie me, if you have the courage of a man! Go on, untie me! *(Her fury becomes uncontrollable.)*

LUIS FERRER *(Out of breath)*: It's best we understand each other, ma'am. Your screams are nothing but whispers here, not even that.

JOANNA: Why don't you kill me?

LUIS FERRER: You fight like the devil himself. I only wish I *could* kill you! But now I understand everything. How could you ever govern if you don't even believe in God?

JOANNA: If you want me to cooperate, call in the people of Tordesillas and let them see that I'm a prisoner. All I ask is that you show them exactly how you treat me. At such a time, I'll be as meek as a lamb. And, while you're at it, you might call in the grandees of Spain to be witnesses to their own treachery and cowardice. And then no word of complaint will pass my lips. Instead, I'll spit on the masks they wear for faces!

LUIS FERRER: You're beginning to fill me with horror. I can't think what might have happened to this glorious Empire if it had been left in your hands!

JOANNA: Well, for one thing, types like you would've had no opportunity to get rich. There would be no jails, no jailers either.

LUIS FERRER: This woman's bewitched! She's a witch! You *are* going to eat, by God!

JOANNA: You are really grotesque, Ferrer. Oh, my God, not torture ...

(FERRER takes up a funnel and after several attempts forces it into her mouth and empties the contents of a vessel into it.)

LUIS FERRER: Here's your soup, you witch!

JOANNA: Ah! ah! *(She coughs, unable to swallow any more and vomits.)*

LUIS FERRER: And now, you'll change your dress!

JOANNA: Swine!

LUIS FERRER: On top of everything else, we have to take care of your appearance! *(He grasps her by the hair.)* Nobody's going to hear us here! Let's take off these underskirts!

JOANNA: No!

LUIS FERRER: Ha-ha-ha! Embarrassed, are we? *(He starts to fondle her.)* You've been brought to bed a good many times, haven't you? And you've kept your looks. Even your father's new wife, Germaine, is jealous of you. *(He suddenly feels the guilt of a torturer.)* But you're crying... So am I... *(He goes on taking off her clothes.)* Poor little thing, poor little queen. You feel like hitting me, don't you? I deserve it. My God, my God, forgive me. Joanna, Joanna, you are so beautiful still. Your body is the sweetest of temptations. *(He kisses her on the neck.)* Your father is arriving today with his wife, and you must receive them properly: as a queen. Long live Queen Joanna! Long live the Queen of Castile! Ha-ha-ha! *(His laughter echoes into infinity.)*

(Change of lighting and scene. FERDINAND is examining an atlas. CISNEROS enters.)

CISNEROS: Your Majesty, you're back at last! Castile welcomes you!

FERDINAND: Oh, Don Francisco, if only all my subjects were like you!

CISNEROS: I'm but a simple and loyal monk.

FERDINAND: Receive from me the Cardinal's hat with which you now become Primate of Spain and Grand Inquisitor.

CISNEROS: I am honored, sire. And, may I ask, is there any word from the Pope?

FERDINAND: The Pope has been taken prisoner and is busy saying his prayers. That's what he gets for poking his nose in where it's not wanted!

CISNEROS: You've taken him prisoner? Then who is praying for us sinners now?

FERDINAND: Don't you have faith in your own prayers?

CISNEROS: I have so much to be forgiven for. He must be raging like a lion!

FERDINAND: I have him swatting flies with his tail!

CISNEROS: Hasn't he said anything about my beatification?

FERDINAND: Europe is in turmoil. There are some new theories going around about Hell. Mercantilism is dead, and there's a new economic order emerging.

CISNEROS: Europe is always doing strange things.

FERDINAND: Our aim is to preserve Spain, so we must all close ranks here. What would have happened to Spain if I hadn't been King of Aragon when Queen Isabella died?

CISNEROS: All Hell would have broken loose.

FERDINAND: I need a son to bring stability to the country.

CISNEROS: The Flemish faction wouldn't take very kindly to that, not to mention your grandson Charles.

FERDINAND: I need to be reinvigorated.

CISNEROS: But you have no lack of vigor.

FERDINAND: The kind of vigor I need now is the bedroom variety.

CISNEROS: Your Majesty! At your age? What would Queen Isabella say if she could hear you in Heaven?

FERDINAND: All this seems to be sent to punish me.

CISNEROS: In that case, we're done for.

FERDINAND: How about working a little miracle, Francis? You could really show off your abilities.

CISNEROS: Show off my abilities by working against the Almighty and Queen Isabella?

FERDINAND: I beg of you, Don Francisco, with tears in my eyes...

CISNEROS: You place me in a very awkward position. I have to consider what will count towards my beatification. I've already made it rain one afternoon in Villaumbrales, and that was some downpour. And I made the statue of Our Lady cry real tears in Granada, when the Moors refused to go to confession. Then I caused the death of the French Cardinal Besacon with a serving of poisoned mushrooms when he tried to bring his Erasmian heresies into Spain and I cured the sacristan of Toledo Cathedral of a tumor in his armpit.

FERDINAND: If you did this for me, it would mean more than if you were able to rebuild the Cathedral dome itself.

CISNEROS: Well, it's probably not all that difficult! There's a certain witch's spell we might try.

FERDINAND: I don't care how you do it! Just get it done!

CISNEROS: We'll make a brew of bull's testicles and tender cats' eyes, while you stroke the genitals of a she-rabbit.

FERDINAND: I can feel it working already without even having to drink it. It isn't a mortal sin, is it?

CISNEROS: Not in special cases like this, when it's all for the good of the country.

FERDINAND: Let's see if we can do it while Queen Isabella is napping up there.

CISNEROS: That's not very likely! But meanwhile, I'm off to the bullfight. *(As he exits)* Poor King Ferdinand! What a martyr's life he lives!

(ISABELLA enters at this moment.)

ISABELLA: God has bestowed many blessings on me in Heaven, but I can't enjoy them because of the view from my window upon the world.

FERDINAND *(Dumbfounded)*: Isabella! What a glorious vision! I must be touched by God's grace!

ISABELLA: Oh, come off it, Ferdinand. You're doing exactly what I would've expected of you. You can't touch anything without making a mess of it. Here I am in Heaven, but I couldn't feel worse if I were down in the Inferno with Dante!

FERDINAND: But don't they say that the joy of Heaven consists of not having to look at what's happening here on Earth?

ISABELLA: That's only for the very sinful souls who've passed on. When you leave behind a feather-brained husband as I did, they give you a window and a bridge of sighs to make the return trip back to earth.

FERDINAND: You must do an awful lot of sighing.

ISABELLA: You ought to be ashamed of yourself.

FERDINAND: Isabella, let me pinch you to make sure this is not just a dream.

ISABELLA: Hands off! I am a blessed spirit, and you are still a body that can be roused to passion!

FERDINAND: There's nothing my body would like better.

ISABELLA: What did you say?

FERDINAND: Things aren't the same without you. I'm terribly lonely.

ISABELLA: You miss the way I used to spoil you, but your main trouble is that your conscience won't let you sleep. A hungry wolf has made its home in the very part of you where sin resides, inflaming your wretched soul.

FERDINAND: Oh, Isabella, if you only knew.

ISABELLA: You needn't say any more. I know it all. You always came begging to me and I gave you honey when I should have given you a cold shower. My heart was open to everything and sometimes we made mistakes that I wouldn't make today.

FERDINAND (He never misses an opportunity): Do you happen to know if certain prayers, coming from Archbishop Cisneros, have been officially received?

ISABELLA: Yes, they have.

FERDINAND: Well?

ISABELLA: The Moorish miracles are invalid.

FERDINAND: But I've done everything in the name of Spain.

ISABELLA: Everything? Does that include drinking the testicles of a bull, you filthy swine? You're nothing but a cesspool of passions named the Playboy of Aragon!

FERDINAND: I can't help it.

ISABELLA: And what about the marriage to the French woman?

FERDINAND: Well, I admit Germaine is French, but she *is a* Catholic.

ISABELLA: No matter! She's *French!*

FERDINAND: Not a day passes that I don't sigh and feel my heart will burst with pain over the sea of grief that I have swallowed since you left us abandoned like orphans to the judgment of history. I've struggled as best I could, but your daughter Joanna hasn't helped a bit.

ISABELLA: With Cisneros there, presiding over the whole mess. I've had it with your partying and promiscuity.

FERDINAND: Are you going to help with a miracle?

ISABELLA: What a hypocrite you are! You expect a miracle? Instead of looking after Joanna and making Spain a sheaf of nations, all firmly bound to one another, you've become the perfect Machiavellian prince. Ambition has been your ruin, Ferdinand, and you have disappointed Our Lady, the Holy Patroness of Spain. Give our daughter Joanna her life back, and we'll all be grateful. Remember! The Patroness of Spain refuses to be French!

(Change of scene and lighting. We are in Arcos, where Joanna was immensely happy before being transferred by her father to Tordesillas in the charge of Luis Ferrer. The light comes up first on the radiantly beautiful figure of JOANNA.)

OANNA *(In a tired voice)*: What do you want of me, Father?

FERDINAND: All I want is to see you, my dear child, and to bring Germaine, who would like to touch you.

JOANNA: You shouldn't have come. I can accept your marriage, but not the shameless motives behind it.

FERDINAND: I am only a man, Joanna.

JOANNA: As to that, I agree, and I'm glad you are.

FERDINAND: The doctors say that you're an admirable female and that there's no other woman in Spain who has given birth so many times or so easily.

JOANNA: What game is this? I won't allow anyone to touch me!

FERDINAND: You are strangely lucid, Joanna.

JOANNA: If *you* were shut away within these four walls, Father, you would become strangely lucid too.

FERDINAND: You take a weight off my shoulders when you say that you find peace and quiet within these walls.

JOANNA: These walls are eternity. What would my mother say if she could see us now, talking so solemnly.

FERDINAND: Don't bring up the dead, however dear they may be. Your mother is now enjoying her eternal rest.

JOANNA: I can't bring myself to wish the same for you.

FERDINAND: Joanna, your mother is blessed with the presence of God. I have it on good authority. They've made her captain of the heavenly host! I know, because I'm in direct communication with her.

JOANNA: Father, you're not talking to a stranger! You can't deceive me any more. You can't deceive anyone any more, not even yourself! Not to mention the grandees of Spain, whose numbers are diminishing as time goes by and who are becoming more and more at odds with you.

FERDINAND: That's just gossip put out by people who would like to see Spain fail.

JOANNA: They are your subjects.

FERDINAND: The ones who refuse to pay taxes, especially the jealous ones, are looking longingly in your direction. This is one of the reasons why I've come to Arcos, where I know you've been very happy. But reasons of state must come before personal comfort. Such is the love I feel for you, Joanna, that I have decided to send you away from Arcos, to avoid reprisals. I don't trust certain fanatics: they might make an attempt on your life.

JOANNA: I'm happy here. I can go in and out, play with the children. Little Ferdy is five now, and Katherine, the pretty darling, is six months old. I have no fear of anyone.

FERDINAND: My secret service agents tell me that you're not safe here.

JOANNA: If that is so, the people to be feared are your secret agents. You'll never persuade me otherwise. Everyone comes to see me here. The Admiral of Castile was here yesterday, accompanied by the Duke of Alba.

FERDINAND *(Perturbed)*: Oh! May one enquire the reason for their visit, Joanna?

JOANNA: Oh, it was just to see me, just to see how I was.

FERDINAND: Did they ask a lot of questions? Did they get you to talk to them?

JOANNA: Of course, Father. I'm not a deaf-mute.

FERDINAND: But you are at times a little absent-minded.

JOANNA: I only remember what I want to.

FERDINAND: What did you talk about?

JOANNA: We made a joint evaluation of the political and economic situation of our country.

FERDINAND: You mean, of Spain.

JOANNA: Of the whole of the Spanish state. They were obviously impressed with me and paid me a lot of compliments too. The Duke of Alba is quite a flirt!

FERDINAND *(Alerted by her words, he reacts like the politician he is)*: You mustn't trust anyone, Joanna. Not even the Duke of Alba or the Admiral. You are in danger here, Joanna. It would be better for you to be moved to Tordesillas.

JOANNA *(Backing away, terrified)*: To Tordesillas? In Tordesillas there are hardly any windows; from the outside it looks like a penitentiary. Father, I need sunshine; I need to be able to gather the first lilies and fill my mouth with blackberries and take the children for walks. I—I haven't done anything so wicked as to deserve being imprisoned in such a place.

FERDINAND: Your life is in jeopardy in Arcos.

JOANNA: My life wouldn't be worth living within those dreary walls. I don't care if my life is in danger. I would gladly give my life just to be able to enjoy it with my children.

FERDINAND: I've decided, also, that it's best for little Ferdinand to come to live with me.

JOANNA: With you? But he's only five years old!

FERDINAND: Children must be instructed from a very early age, and even more so if they have royal responsibilities.

JOANNA: What game is this you're playing, Father? What subtle web are you weaving now like a great big poisonous spider? Why don't you tell me the truth?

FERDINAND: A faithful servant of mine, Luis Ferrer, will take care of your slightest need there in Tordesillas.

JOANNA: No-o-o-o! I tell you I'll never go to Tordesillas, never! To get me there, you'll have to drag me or put me in chains! But right now I want the truth from you. The truth is that you're afraid of me, so you not only shut me away in Tordesillas but you take my son hostage too, just to be on the safe side. *That's* the truth, the plain truth. You are not a father! You're riddled through and through with ambition. You're a fugitive from your own conscience. No, I don't want to see you! You're the most contemptible of beings! Mother, Mother, help me! He's going to lock me away in Tordesillas and kidnap little Ferdinand. Mother!

FERDINAND: Joanna, Joanna! What are you saying? You see, you're having one of your fits again. You are insane, insane!

JOANNA: You're afraid they'll come and ask me to be Queen of Castile! You're afraid I'll take back what is mine, mine, mine!

FERDINAND: My soldiers are surrounding Arcos at this very moment. I've nothing more to say. I don't want a scene. You'll be better off than any queen in Tordesillas. *(He exits.)*

JOANNA: Oh no, there is no God, there is no God, no God. There are things, objects, persons who come and go, who make gestures with their hands and overpower me. Here, that's all there is. God doesn't exist.

ISABELLA: Yes, He does, Joanna, just as Jesus exists. And there are beautiful beings like you, Joanna, who will one day become models of conduct for the rest of humanity.

JOANNA: I don't want to be anybody's model of anything! No, I don't understand, Mother.

ISABELLA: Look, my child, I've learned a lot since I died and saw the last of your father. Jesus Christ Himself came down to remedy the ignorance of mortal beings, and, in a way, He had to accept ignorance, too, when He took on mortal flesh, just as He accepted sin in order to redeem us from it. And He tried to do so through the madness of the Cross and through some unsophisticated apostles whom He chose for their simplicity, not their cleverness. The examples He gave them were the childen, the lilies of the field, a grain of mustard seed and the birds, all simple creatures, unschooled, living by instinct, free from worries and cares. Only Lucifer is clever, like your father.

JOANNA: Mommy, what do you mean? This is not like you.

ISABELLA: At the moment we spend our evenings reading *In Praise of Folly* by Erasmus, and then we sing some very pretty songs. To finish up they let us play a game with the Child Jesus. Oh my darling, foolish girl, I love you.

JOANNA: Take me away! Take me away with you!

ISABELLA: I only wish I could! *(She disappears.)*

(Music. Sounds of iron doors clanging as they are violently opened and closed. JOANNA'S body seems to have shrunk. She looks like a little old lady, clear-headed and angry. Steps can be heard approaching. The MARQUIS OF DENIA appears, played by the same actor who played FRIAR MARTIN and LUIS FERRER.)

JOANNA: Friar Martin, Friar Martin, you've come again at last! I've been waiting to give you a piece of my mind.

DENIA: Forgive me, Your Highness. My name is Don Bernardo de Sandoval y Rojas, Marquis of Denia, sent by your son, King Charles, to be your most humble servant.

JOANNA: Ah, another one? I must be very important to be the object of so much concern to so many people! But I fear this concern is not good for my health. Well, well, Mr. Denia.

DENIA: Marquis of Denia, Your Highness.

JOANNA: Well, Marquis, or whatever ... you will tell my son Charles...

DENIA: His Majesty King Charles, Your Highness.

JOANNA: All right, tell the King from me that on top of coming here only when he has something to gain, he has robbed me of my mother's jewels.

DENIA: Are you calling the King a thief, Your Highness?

JOANNA: Who are you to question me? What do you know about it? Do you think that the King's servants are the only ones capable of stealing? Well, you can tell him that he should be ashamed to go around emptying the pockets of honest folk. And tell him that he has done enough catechizing around Europe; it's time he took care of Spain, for this is where he'll find the noblest hearts.

DENIA: His Majesty has ordered me to come and has given me his total confidence. He is very worried about you. Gossip has reached his ears that you sleep in the nude!

JOANNA: I've always been a source of worry to someone, Denia. I've been worrying everyone for nearly thirty years. It gives them something to talk about. Let's see, my friend. Haven't you ever tried sleeping in the nude in the summer?

DENIA: I, Your Highness? I beg you to be careful what you say.

JOANNA: I might have known! Here we go again with another moralizing prude. Try it, my friend, and you'll see it makes you feel like a feather floating in the breeze, way up high. But, of course, before you can do that, you have to know how to enjoy being alone. There are people who run from the phantom of loneliness; they've no idea what they're missing. No one is free unless he is really alone. I must confess, Marquis, that I am alone against my will. As a child I was very, very sociable, and I loved sharing my freedom with everyone else, until they realized, and then they shut me away and made me play by myself. Why should it surprise anyone now if I do whatever I like? They are just a bunch of killjoys. Yes, Denia, tell my son, King Charles, what I have said, and tell my grandson Philip too. He doesn't seem too healthy, poor thing.

DENIA: Ma'am, your grandson Philip is also grieved to see you looking like this.

JOANNA: Then let him look the other way! The only one who should be worried here is me, and I'm not worried. So, take my advice: try sleeping in the nude. And encourage your wife to do the same.

DENIA: Your Highness!

JOANNA: Oh, my Philip and I often used to do it and we had a great time, believe you me, Mr. Denia.

DENIA: Marquis, Your Highness.

JOANNA: Would you believe, marquis, that I still think fondly of my Philip in spite of all that happened?

DENIA: And what about making the sign of the Cross before you go to bed?

JOANNA: You can tell my grandson Philip that the two things are not incompatible.

DENIA: Surely you don't mean that one can pray in the nude?

JOANNA: The Gospels have nothing whatever to say against it.

DENIA: But the Pope certainly has.

JOANNA: And what does the Pope know about it? He's never read Erasmus.

DENIA: Ah, yes, I was just coming to that. *(He behaves as if he had just won a dialectical victory over JOANNA.)* I was indeed just coming to that. Your son and grandson have good reason to be worried. I feel ashamed for you, ma'am. To think that the mother of the King of Spain has actually read Erasmus of Rotterdam instead of soaking up the words of the great teacher, John of Avila! It goes beyond belief! Your Highness should immediately make the sign of the Cross over your lips!

JOANNA: You are intent upon torturing me. Not one of you understands anything. Erasmus is read even in Heaven; my mother has told me so herself! You can tell the King that his grandmother is sorry now for having burned the Koran, and that the tower of the Cathedral in Seville is Moorish, whether he likes it or not!

DENIA: Get down on your knees and repent for all your sins, ma'am!

JOANNA: You came here just to let me have it, didn't you?

DENIA: I had heard many things about you and your behavior, but your disorder goes beyond mere insanity. There is something demoniacal about you. You have cut yourself off from the body of Christ!

JOANNA: That's enough, my lord marquis! I reject what you say! I haven't cut myself off from anything except a herd of silly donkeys who think their asinine braying is pleasing to God, but they are mistaken!

DENIA: Ma'am, with such thoughts you cannot be in state of grace with God.

JOANNA: I love God.

DENIA: Your Highness, you must confess your sins.

JOANNA: The last thing I need is to tell my secrets to some fool.

DENIA *(The politician in him becomes suddenly alert)*: Your secrets, you say? What do you mean?

JOANNA: I have my secrets, sir.

DENIA: In your case, that is very dangerous. Have you been in contact, by any chance, with Juan Padilla, the leader of the rebellion?

JOANNA: Look here, Denia! I am sick and tired of all your suspicions.

DENIA *(As a politician)*: Your Highness, Castile is going through a very delicate phase of political disturbances which have been shamefully exploited by those who would promote war between the social classes. It's like temporary rash on the body politic, but it will pass because it leads nowhere. These rebels, ma'am, are from the lower classes and they hate your son King Charles with all their hearts. They seek nothing less than the destruction of Spain.

JOANNA: Good heavens, Denia. What villains! They sound like characters from an outdated novel. But I still can't forgive my son for having stolen my mother's earrings.

DENIA: Your Highness, say you repent, once and for all, of all your sins. Your mind seems to swing like the clapper of a bell inside your head. Renounce Satan and all his works.

JOANNA: I refuse.

(DENIA loses all control of himself and chains her, with some difficulty, to the same chair which previously served LUIS FERRER as an instrument of torture.)

OANNA: A-a-a-ah! You are hurting me! Don't! Don't!

DENIA: Have you been in contact with Juan Padilla? Yes or no?

JOANNA: I haven't been in contact with anyone. Let me go! You are hurting me!

DENIA: You're lying! You're hiding something! You will sign a document in which you will condemn any action questioning the legitimacy of the governors appointed by your son, King Charles.

JOANNA: Sign? In what capacity?

DENIA: As Queen of Castile.

JOANNA: I don't know whether this is real or just a dream. What kind of perverse, strange world is this which twists everything to suit the need of the moment? I... I am a human being, not a puppet to be worked with strings. I, my lord Marquis of Denia, am tired of it all. All I ask is to be left in peace, in peace, I say!

(The torturer relents a little.)

DENIA: Your Highness, Spain requires it of you. It is the best service you can perform for her cause.

JOANNA: Spain, Spain... All I have ever wished for has been the good of Spain! One day, long ago, they sent me to Flanders for the sake of Spain. For the sake of Spain I was married there, and for the sake of Spain I am now shut away from sight. I'm sorry, Denia, but I won't sign anything.

DENIA: You are worse than any viper! You are the worst enemy Spain could have!

JOANNA: Leave me alone, and untie me immediately!

DENIA: Not until you sign here! *(He tortures her.)*

JOANNA: A-a-a-ah! Help! Help me, someone!

(The scene changes. Sounds of horses, voices, violence, gunshots.)

ENIA: What's going on?

VOICES: Long live the rebelion! Long live the Queen! Castile for Queen Joanna!

GUARD'S VOICE: Sir! Tordesillas is in the hands of the rebels!

(DENIA lashes out at JOANNA in a fury.)

DENIA: You bitch! So that was your secret, was it?

JOANNA: Help! Help! I don't know anything about it, anything at all! Help me!

(The noise of shouting and horses' hooves is deafening. The MARQUIS OF DENIA picks up his weapons just as JUAN PADILLA enters.)

PADILLA: Don't move, my lord marquis! Take one step and you are dead! *(He goes towards Joanna who is gazing around, stunned, not knowing what is going on)* Your Majesty, you are free!

JOANNA: Free? Who are you? What is the meaning of these weapons? *(Looking at DENIA, and speaking in a whisper.)* Are they going to kill me?

PADILLA: You need have no fear for your life, Your Majesty. I am Juan Padilla, the son of López Padilla, who was Captain General under the late Queen, your mother. He had the courage to defend you once before when you were imprisoned while your husband was still alive.

JOANNA *(Gently placing her hand over his mouth)*: Hush! Say no more. My husband loved me.

PADILLA: I have no doubt he did, Your Majesty.

JOANNA *(Calmly)*: Your father was a man of noble character, Juan Padilla. I remember his courage as an old man when he served in Parliament as the people's representative from Toledo.

PADILLA: And now it's my turn, Your Majesty, and I have the people of Toledo behind me, awaiting your orders!

JOANNA: What a beautiful gesture! And how unusual. I'm sure my mother must be watching you, Padilla, from her window in Heaven, with tears in her eyes. *(She gazes at him lovingly.)* How you've grown! I still remember how you used to accompany your father when you were a child, on visits to the country. You used to stay behind with me—I was by then a teenager—and I played at being your mother! No, you mustn't kneel! Rise, Juan Padilla, I'm no longer anybody!

PADILLA: Your Majesty, I wish to speak to you alone.

DENIA: Don't take any notice, my lady. He's trying to trick you.

PADILLA: Marquis, if you value your life, leave this room at once!

JOANNA: It is I who give orders here!

PADILLA: Forgive me, Your Majesty.

JOANNA *(Glaring at DENIA)*: Leave us!

DENIA: I shall report immediately to the King.

PADILLA: Give him all the details!

(DENIA hurries out.)

JOANNA: Sit down. You must excuse the way in which I have to receive you.

PADILLA: So this is the way they have repaid you, Your Majesty.

JOANNA: I don't complain about being poor, Juan, but I do resent the limits on my physical freeedom. They hardly ever allow me to go to Mass, and then they say that I'm a heretic.

PADILLA: Your Majesty, time is precious. The townships are in revolt. Castile won't put up with any more injustices. While your father was alive, the discontent was muffled, though it existed even then, but with the arrival of your son Charles and this crowd of leeches who came with him from abroad, the situation has become unbearable. So much pillaging and robbery! *(JOANNA nods as if to say: "I know all about it.")* The mainspring of the rebellion is to be found in Toledo and Segovia, the commercial centers, with the enthusiastic support of Madrid, Avila, Salamanca, Medina, Zamora, Toro, Valladolid, Palencia and Leon. We can count on the support of Murcia too, but Andalusia is still in doubt. Your Majesty, there are enough of us to build a powerful new state founded on the will of the people! We have come together in service to Your Majesty and for your defense. Tell us your will and we will carry it out, come what may!

JOANNA: How beautiful, Juan Padilla, how beautiful it all sounds. Tell you my will? What will could I possibly have left when I've been dispossessed of my daughter Katherine and robbed of my jewels by my own son? But I count the last seventeen years well spent if only because I've been permitted to hear your words which have moved me so. I'm sure that any prisoner would give anything to change places with me. How beautiful, how beautiful everything is, Juan Padilla.

PADILLA: Your Majesty, I understand the emotion of this moment for you, but I'm asking you to do something more: to make decisions here and now. The day will come when history will call you to account.

JOPANNA: Oh, Padilla, you are so naive. Out of sight, out of mind. History will have no trouble burying me beneath the sands of time.

PADILLA: Not all the sand in all the deserts will be enough to bury the name of Joanna of Castile.

JOANNA: If I were younger, Padilla, I would suspect you were courting me. No, Padilla, historians love looking for the misfits who fall through the cracks of history, and with me they'll have a field day! It will be difficult for them to find anyone crazier than me, and I'm sure they'll make the most of it. You know, Padilla, I'm hopelessly out of my mind.

PADILLA: There can be no delay. This is no time for reluctance or nostalgia. Our time is now, Your Majesty.

JOANNA: Padilla, you were born into a new and energetic class of people, full of ideas, whereas I am like an eagle whose wings have been clipped. Is there anything sadder than to see such a majestic creature trailing along on the ground, unable to fly?

PADILLA: It's sadder to give up one's place in history, Your Majesty. There's only one way to rid Spain of these heartless foreigners—by the sword. And you *can* fly if only you'll allow our rebel swords to be your wings.

JOANNA: You may think I'm joking, Padilla, but we've driven so many of them out of Spain at one time or another that I don't think I have the energy left to do it again. The result is always the same: you drive them out and then you're sorry. My mother rues the day she expelled the Jews. But who would have thought that the nobility of Spain would turn out to be a pack of dunces counting on their fingers? Look, Padilla, this country is very odd, and I wouldn't dare to...

PADILLA: Your Majesty, I assure you this time it's absolutely necessary. The foreigners brought here by your son are ruining us!

JOANNA: Padilla, you break my heart. If you wish, I'll appoint you Captain General. After that, God's will be done!

(DENIA enters in a panic, carrying a crucifix in his hand.)

DENIA: Your Highness, Your Highness! *(He looks at PADILLA out of the corner of his eye.)* Your grandson Philip has just arrived.

JOANNA: What? My grandson? Heaven help us, he'll have us all reciting the rosary.

DENIA: And doing penance.

JOANNA: How right you are! And my knees are not up to doing penance just now.

DENIA: Prince Philip looks very pale and upset. They say that a shoemaker in Llerena has been at court predicting the end of the world this afternoon!

JOANNA: Well? So what?

DENIA: Doesn't it matter to you?

JOANNA: It's all the same to me.

DENIA: We could all go to Hell!

JOANNA: Denia, that's a problem for each one of us to deal with on our own.

PADILLA: Marquis, stop this nonsense. If your intention was to scare Her Majesty with your announcement, you've failed. And if you're trying to frighten me, just be thankful that I haven't run you through with this sword!

JOANNA: Hush, Padilla! Marquis, go and tell my grandson Philip that I've no wish to see him and that I, for one, will be immensely relieved if the world does come to an end this afternoon.

DENIA: She's crazy, absolutely crazy. But, what's worse, she's possessed by the devil.

(DENIA exits, making signs of the Cross and all manner of other gestures.)

JOANNA: For each of us, Padilla, there comes a day when we must define ourselves, and apparently today is the day for me. I can't spare you this. I know that I'm going to disappoint you, Padilla, but I've made up my mind. I want to go on being crazy, Juan Padilla, forgive me. Erasmus once said that making mistakes was unfortunate, but not making mistakes was even worse. Another woman would have seized the blazing torch and thrown it at her own son. To accomplish what you want to do, Padilla, you must be ready to kill, and I wouldn't know how. I'm just a crazy woman, and crazy folk don't understand about killing. Padilla, would you play a game with me? Perhaps madness is contagious.

PADILLA: I don't know, Your Majesty. Remember that the sane folk always outnumber the crazy ones.

JOANNA: It's a child's game that I used to play for hours with my daughter Katherine. It's very simple. You play it on one leg. You mustn't move, or laugh, or speak. *(Gradually the light fades from PADILLA.)* There's no room in history for feelings. If feelings get involved, the result is always the same. Look what happened to me! There's no room anywhere for anything except the love of material things, and if you don't go along, they tell you you're insane.

(Music.)

ISABELLA: Joanna, Joanna...

JOANNA: Mommy, will you teach me that beautiful song that you and all the saints sing together, up there in heaven?

ISABELLA: Oooh! We sing all sorts of things, even songs from the twentieth century. Listen!

CHILDREN'S VOICES:
> I would like to be
> as tall as the moon,
> as tall as the moon
> as tall as the moon

JOANNA: I would like to be as tall as the moon...

(The curtain slowly falls.)

THE END

Emma Penella as Queen Isabella and Lola Herrera as Joanna in the original 1983 production of *Juana del amor hermoso*, directed by Angel Ruggiero.

CRITICAL REACTION TO THE PRODUCTION IN MADRID

Manuel Martínez Mediero... lifts his protagonist, Joanna of Castile, off the pages of history, and endows her with the soul of a woman of our times. His play, *Juana del amor hermoso (A Love Too Beautiful)*, is, I believe... one of the fundamental dramatic texts of the Spanish theater of today.

>Antonio Corencia
>Theater Director, Madrid
>*Primer Acto* (Madrid) 197, January 1983

With both a serious sense of history and a facility for evoking laughter, this play by Martínez Mediero invents a new kind of dramatic unity.

>F. García Pavón
>Author and critic, Madrid
>*El espectador y la crítica* (Madrid), 1983

The plot of *Juana del amor hermoso (A Love Too Beautiful)* draws us into the story of Joanna the Mad... It is a tragicomic vision in which Isabella and Ferdinand play the comic roles and Joanna is the tragic character.

>José Monleón
>Theater critic, Madrid
>*Primer Acto* (Madrid) 197, January 1983

ABOUT THE TRANSLATOR

Hazel Cazorla is Professor of Spanish and Director of the Spanish Program at the University of Dallas. A native of England, she received her degrees in Modern Languages from Oxford University where she was also active in the theater. After working as a translator in London, she moved to Spain and eventually to Texas, where she combined directing university theatrical productions in Spanish with her academic interests. Her publications include numerous articles on the contemporary Spanish theater and an edition of Antonio Gala's *Los verdes campos del Eden*.

TRANSLATOR'S ACKNOWLEDGMENTS

I acknowledge a long-standing debt of gratitude to Martha Halsey, infinitely patient and efficacious editor of this series, and to Phyllis Zatlin for her invaluable advice in the preparation of this translation. My thanks go also to Judy Kelly, Professor of Drama at the University of Dallas, for her cooperation and interest in the performance of plays by Spanish authors. I also thank Robert Dixon for his conscientious attention in preparing the camera-ready copy for this volume.

ESTRENO: CONTEMPORARY SPANISH PLAYS SERIES
General Editor: Martha T. Halsey

No. 1 Jaime Salom: *Bonfire at Dawn* (*Una hoguera al amanecer*)
Translated by Phyllis Zatlin. 1992.   IBSN: 0-9631212-0-0

No. 2 José López Rubio: *In August We Play the Pyrenees* (*Celos del aire*)
Translated by Marion P. Holt. 1992.   IBSN: 0-9631212-1-9

No. 3 Ramón del Valle-Inclán: *Savage Acts: Four Plays* (*Ligazón, La rosa de papel, La cabeza del Bautista, Sacrilegio*) Translated by Robert Lima. 1993.   IBSN: 0-9631212-2-7

No. 4 Antonio Gala: *The Bells of Orleans* (*Los buenos días perdidos*)
Translated by Edward Borsoi. 1993.   IBSN: 0-9631212-3-5

No. 5 Antonio Buero-Vallejo: *The Music Window* (*Música cercana*)
Translated by Marion P. Holt. 1994.   IBSN: 0-9631212-4-3

No. 6 Paloma Pedrero: *Parting Gestures: Three by Pedrero* (*El color de agosto, La noche dividida, Resguardo personal*) Translated by Phyllis Zatlin. 1994.   IBSN: 0-9631212-5-1

No. 7 Ana Diosdado: *Yours for the Asking* (*Usted también podrá disfrutar de ella*)
Translated by Patricia W. O'Connor. 1995.   IBSN: 0-9631212-6-X

No. 8 Manuel Martínez Mediero: *A Love Too Beautiful* (*Juana del amor hermoso*)
Translated by Hazel Cazorla. 1995.   IBSN: 0-9631212-7-8

SUBSCRIPTION/ORDER FORM

Check one:

_____ Standing order for play series. (May be cancelled at any time if desired.)
$6.00 including postage, to be billed when you receive your copy.

_____ Individual play/s. List titles and quantities below:

_____ | _____ | _____

_____ | _____ | _____

_____ | _____ | _____

Please include payment at $5.00 per copy, postpaid. Special Cincinnati conference price.

Name and address: _____

_____

Mail to: ESTRENO
350 N. Burrowes Bldg.
University Park, PA 16802 USA

Telephone: 814/865-1122
FAX: 814/863-7944

ESTRENO:
CUADERNOS DEL TEATRO
ESPAÑOL CONTEMPORANEO

Published at Penn State University
Martha Halsey, Ed.
Phillis Zatlin, Assoc. Ed.

A journal featuring play texts of previously unpublished works from contemporary Spain, interviews withplaywrights, directors, and critics, and extensive critical studies in both Spanish and English.

Plays published have included texts by Buero-Vallejo, Sastre, Arrabal, Gala, Nieva, Salom, Martín Recuerda, Olmo, Martínez Mediero, F. Cabal, P. Pedrero and Onetti. The journal carries numerous photographs of recent play performances in Spain and elsewhere, including performances in translation.

Also featured are an annual bibliography, regular book reviews, and critiques of the recent theater season, as well as a round table in which readers from both the U. S. and Spain share information and engage in lively debates.

ESTRENO also publishes a series of translations of contemporary Spanish plays which may be subscribed to separately.

- -

Please mail to: ESTRENO
350 N. Burrowes Bldg.
University Park, PA 16802
USA.

Individual subscriptions are $14.00 and institutional subscriptions, $26.00 for the calendar year.

Name   _____

Address   _____

_____